Dialectical Materialism

DIALECTICAL
MATERIALISM

V. G. AFANSAYEV

INTERNATIONAL PUBLISHERS, New York

© 1987 by Progress Publishers

©1987 by International Publishers Co., Inc.
1st printing, revised edition, 1987

Manufactured in the United States of America

Library of Congress Cataloging-in-Publication Data

Afanas'ev, Viktor Grigor'evich
 Dialectical materialism

Rev. translation of the 1st pt. of: Osnovy filosofskikh znaniǐ
1. Dialectical materialism. 2. Philosophy, Marxist. I. Title.
B809.8A3273   1987   146'.32   87-3419
ISBN 0-7178-0656-1 (pbk.)

CONTENTS

Dialectical Materialism

TO THE READER

This book is intended for those who are beginning to study Marxist-Leninist philosophy.

What does one gain from studying Marxist philosophy? Marxist philosophy* is a *harmonious system of man's views of the surrounding world, the laws of its development and ways of cognising it.* A study of philosophy, therefore, provides us with a coherent idea of the world and its development, of man's place in the world and whether he can cognise and transform it, why the life of society changes and how best to organise it, and so forth.

What is the practical significance of these general questions and how do they directly benefit man's life and work?

The practical significance of Marxist philosophy is enormous. Being a component part of Marxism-Leninism, Marxist philosophy renders invaluable assistance to all progressive forces in their struggle for humanity's better future by disclosing the more general laws of the development of nature, society and thinking, and showing the need and inevitability of socialist revolution and the triumph of socialism and communism.

Marxist philosophy offers a truly scientific explanation of nature and society and consequently is a powerful instrument of their revolutionary transformation.

Only the proletariat and its Party are concerned with acquiring a correct knowledge and carrying out a revolutionary transformation of the world. That is why dialectical materialism emerged and is developing as a theoretical, ideological weapon of the proletariat in its struggle against capitalism, for socialism and communism. The philosophy of Marxism is revolutionary in its very essence. Recognising neither immutable social systems nor eternal mainstays of private property, it theoretically proves that the doom of capitalism and the victory of the new socialist, communist society are inevitable.

It is especially important to master Marxist philosophy in our epoch of radical social change and the transition from capitalism to socialism. It helps Marxist parties find their bearings in the very complex conditions of our time, make a scientific analysis of the actual situation and then define the most important tasks and find the most effective ways of attaining them. Should the Marxist political party and its examination of questions base

---

* From the Greek—philosophia meaning love or pursuit of wisdom (phil + sophia).

itself not on dialectics and materialism, the result will be one-sidedness and subjectivism, stagnation of human thought, isolation from life and loss of ability to make the necessary analysis of things and phenomena, revisionist and dogmatist mistakes and erroneous policy. Application of dialectical materialism in practical work and the education of the party functionaries and the broad masses in the spirit of Marxism-Leninism are urgent tasks of the communist and workers' parties.

Marxist philosophy is a powerful theoretical instrument for cognising and transforming the world, but only if applied *creatively and with strict consideration of the concrete historical conditions in which its laws and principles operate.* In order to master Marxist philosophy it is not enough to learn by rote its propositions and conclusions: it is necessary to grasp its essence and to learn to apply it in practice in solving concrete tasks of the revolutionary struggle for peace, democracy, national liberation and socialism.

For ages, people dreamed of a society that would do away with exploitation and all sorts of oppression, and in which a person of labour would use all that one's hands and intellect create, and each member of the great community of working people would live in abundance and happiness. Mankind traversed a long and arduous road of titanic struggle, glorious victories and temporary setbacks before such a society—communism—ceased to be a dream and became an immediate prospect of historical development, a supreme force of our day and age.

The struggle for the victory of communism envisages not only the creation of the material and technical basis and the moulding of communist social relations, but also the all-round development of the human personality. But to be able to do this, a member of society needs more than to be a specialist in one's field. It is important to master the totality of human knowledge, and even more important, to learn to apply it. A person has to acquire a scientific world outlook in order that communist ideas combine organically with communist deeds in one's work and life. In contemporary conditions the shaping of a scientific world outlook on the basis of Marxism-Leninism as a harmonious system of philosophical, economic and sociopolitical views is a matter of primary importance.

The philosophy of Marxism promotes the understanding of the course and prospects of world development and correct grasping of events taking place in the country itself and elsewhere in the world, and convinces people in the just nature of the revolutionary cause and the inevitability of the victory of socialism and communism throughout the world. It mobilises the people for the struggle against the reactionary imperialist ideology and the survivals of the past, helps to perceive and surmount the difficulties.

Marxist philosophy cultivates a broad and correct world outlook in a person and trains each to discern the importance of seemingly insignificant things. It stimulates thought, makes it more flexible and incisive, and hostile to stagnation and routine; it imbues people with the valuable sense of the new. This is most important, for in our age of unprecedented scientific and technical progress and the subjugation of the atom, in our age of electricity, automatic systems and space exploration it is impossible to do without an incisive, resourceful mind.

Marxist philosophy shows the scientist the correct road. It is a beacon for the writer and artist in their creative endeavours and helps them deeply and vividly to portray the greatness of our age.

Knowledge of Marxist philosophy is essential for progressive young people in all countries because it helps them to gain political maturity and cultivate integrity, staunchness and courage in the struggle against national and social oppression. Without these qualities it is impossible to build a bright future.

In a word, those who fight for national liberation and social emancipation, who build socialism, those who seek the truth, who want to probe the secrets of the universe and life ought to master the invincible Marxist-Leninist teaching and its life-asserting philosophy.

Life repudiates all sorts of nihilistic ideological conceptions invented in the West, according to which we are now witnessing either the general decline in the role and significance of philosophy and ideology in the system of scientific cognition and practical activity, or the automatic "removal" of all ideological problems and precepts by the very course of scientific and technical progress, the mathematisation of science and the introduction of cybernetics and modelling methods, or the "inability" of Marxist philosophy to meet the "challenge" of new successes, new problems of modern natural science, etc.

In actual fact the very nature of philosophical knowledge rules out such assessments because it is rooted in the requirements of social development itself and is designed to identify and develop eternal values and problems: the more common, universal conceptions of the world, of its past and future, the more general foundations and principles of life, cognisance and practical activity, the meaning of human existence, social progress, development of mankind, etc.

Philosophical knowledge is not a fruit of idle reflections of dilettantes, but a form of social consciousness which reflects the advances of scientific and social progress, the ideals and world outlook of different classes, social contradictions and conflicts in the given country and in the given epoch. That was why Marx called philosophy the "intellectual quintessence" of its time, "the living soul of culture".*

In 1978 the 16th World Philosophic Congress was held in Düsseldorf. It was attended by more than one thousand scientists, including mathematicians, physicists, chemists, astronomers and biologists from many countries. The choice of the main theme of the congress—"The Philosophy and Ideological Problems of Modern Science"—was indicative of the appreciation of the importance of philosophy for concrete natural and social sciences and recognition of the untenability of counterposing philosophy to natural sciences, and emphasised the bankruptcy of ideological nihilism.

In fact discussions at the congress went far beyond the limits of the main theme. It examined not only basic ideological problems of contemporary science, but also of contemporary social life; philosophical interpretations of our epoch, prospects of mankind's development in conditions of the struggle between the two opposite world systems— socialism and capitalism—and problems of their peaceful coexistence.

Life shows that the mounting complexity and intensification of revolutionary transformations in the world, the acceleration of the scientific and technical progress and the increasing influence of its social consequences imperatively call for a philosophical rethinking of the fundamental problems and patterns of social development and scientific cognisance, and of the ideological orientation of man's spiritual and practical activities.

---

* Karl Marx, "The Leading Article in No. 179 of the *Kölnische-Zeitung*", in: *Karl Marx, Frederick Engels, Collected Works*, Vol. 1, Progress Publishers, Moscow, 1975, p. 195.

INTRODUCTION

CHAPTER I

Philosophy As a Science

As any other science Marxist philosophy has its own subject matter. Before speaking about it, however, let us look into the problems which are solved by Marxist and all other philosophies. The main problem is the *fundamental question of philosophy.*

1. The Fundamental Question of Philosophy. The Antithesis of Materialism and Idealism.

Philosophy is one of the oldest sciences. Many philosophical systems have been developed by the most diverse social classes and groups in different historical conditions and countries. In order to find our bearings in this multitude of philosophical systems, ascertain their scientific value and determine the place that each occupies in the history of philosophical thought, it is necessary in the first place to see how a philosophical system or a philosopher solves the fundamental question of philosophy.

If we look carefully at the surrounding world we shall see that all objects and phenomena are either *material,* or *ideal, spiritual.* Material phenomena embrace everything that *exists objectively,* i.e., *outside of man's consciousness and independently of it* (objects and processes on Earth, the countless bodies of the Universe, etc.). On the other hand, all that *exists in the consciousness* of man and all that comprises the sphere of his mental activity (thoughts, sensations, emotions, etc.), is related to the sphere of the ideal, the spiritual.

How are the material and the spiritual connected? Is the spiritual, the ideal engendered by the material, or vice versa? *It is the nature of this connection, of the relation of consciousness to being, of the spiritual to the material that constitutes the fundamental question of philosophy.*

The relation of consciousness to being is the fundamental question of philosophy because the answer to it determines the solution of all other philosophical problems: the unity of the world, the character of the laws governing its development, the essence of knowledge and ways of cognising the world, etc. Hence, it is impossible to create a philosophical

7

system and draw a picture of the world as a whole without first solving the fundamental question of philosophy.

There are two aspects to this question. The first is the solution of the problem, *what is primary,* matter or consciousness—was it matter that was the source of consciousness—or vice versa. The other aspect answers the question, *is the world cognisable,* can man's reason penetrate the secrets of nature and ascertain the laws of its development.

Pondering the content of the fundamental question of philosophy it is easy to perceive that there can be only two diametrically opposite approaches: to recognise either matter or consciousness as primary. That accounts for the existence of two basic trends in philosophy—materialism and idealism—which appeared a long time ago.

Philosophers who regard *matter as primary* and consciousness as secondary, and as a derivative of matter, are *materialists* (from Latin *materia,* meaning matter). They maintain that matter is eternal, that no one had ever created it and that there are no supernatural forces in the world. As regards consciousness, it is the product of the historical development of matter, a property of that exceptionally complex material body, the human brain.

Philosophers who believe that the *"spirit", or consciousness is primary* are *idealists.* They maintain that consciousness existed prior to matter and brought it into being, and that it is the primary foundation of everything that exists. Idealists are divided on the question *what kind of consciousness* "creates" the world. The so-called *subjective idealists* assert that the world is "created" by the consciousness of the individual—the subject. *Objective idealists,* on the other hand, insist that the world is "created" by some kind of an objective (superindividual) consciousness. Though in different philosophical systems this objective consciousness is called either an "absolute idea", or "universal will", etc., it is easy to discern that it presupposes God.

The views of the philosophers on the solution of the other aspect of the fundamental question of philosophy are likewise divided.

The *world is knowable,* assert the materialists. Man's knowledge of the world is trustworthy, his reason can penetrate the internal nature of things and cognise their essence.

Many idealists *deny the knowability of the world.* They are called *agnostics* (from Greek agnostos—unknown, unknowable, not knowing). Other idealists, even if they believe that the world is knowable, in reality distort the essence of knowledge. They claim that man cognises his own thoughts, emotions (subjective idealists), or a mystic "idea", a "universal spirit" (objective idealists), and not the objective world, nature.

Whom Do Materialism and Idealism Serve

Materialism, in its contemporary, Marxist-Leninist form is a progressive scientific world outlook. It correctly portrays the world and is a true ally of science and man's practical activity on the basis of which it itself has arisen and is developing.

Materialism has always been the world outlook of the advanced classes and sections of society interested in promoting the wellbeing of the people, the progress of mankind and its economic and cultural development. In the slaveowning society materialism was used by the democratic strata to fight against the aristocracy, the upper crust of the slave-owners. In the period of the rise of capitalism it was an ideological weapon of the bourgeoisie in its battles against the feudal lords and the church. Today materialism is a mighty weapon of the progressive part of mankind in its struggle against imperialist reactionary forces.

Idealism is at cross-purposes with a scientific interpretation of the world. Like religion it places supernatural forces in the centre of the picture of the world and essentially is a masked, refined form of religion. The reason is obvious: idealism cloaks the religious myth about the divine creation of the world in subtle philosophical verbiage. Idealism is particularly dangerous because it tries to pose as a science and prey upon one's reason, not limiting itself to blind faith, as religion does.

As a rule, idealism serves the reactionary forces of society in their struggle against the progressive social forces. The exploiters always tried to use idealism and religion to enslave the working people spiritually and to justify and reinforce their domination. Today, too, the moribund capitalist system tries to rely on idealism and religion.

By preaching humility and submission and promising paradise religion distracts the attention of the working people from crucial social problems and from fighting against exploitation and poverty, for peace, democracy, national liberation and socialism.

Idealism, in effect, does the same thing. Denying the objective existence of the world and regarding it as a product of consciousnees alone, it attributes all social contradictions and suffering, all the vices of capitalism to the delusions of the people and their moral failings. Thus, like religion, it diverts the working people from fighting against the forces of imperialist reaction.

There is a kinship between idealism and religion, but they should not be fully identified. And although some idealists made a certain contribution to the development of philosophical thought, on the whole, all of them gave a distorted picture of the world.

The achievements in science and practical experience demonstrated idealism's insolvency a long time ago. Yet idealist views are still popular in capitalist countries chiefly because this is in the class interests of the exploiters. The exploiting classes need idealism as a means of fighting against materialism and as an instrument of the spiritual enslavement of the working people. That explains why they support and spread idealism in every way.

Since there are no exploiters in socialist society, there are no people interested in implanting idealism and no one disseminates it there. The scientific, materialist world outlook prevails under socialism.

We have established that philosophers are divided into materialists and idealists, depending on how they solve the fundamental question of philosophy. But as they draw a picture of the world each of them unavoidably employs a specific *method* of cognition. What, then, is a method?

2. The Concept of Method. Dialectics and Metaphysics

In the process of acquiring knowledge and in their practical activities people set themselves definite goals and tasks. But to set a goal or to formulate a task does not mean that it will be accomplished. It is very important to find the right road to the goal and effective methods for fulfilling the task. The road to the attainment of a goal, the aggregate of definite principles and ways of theoretical study and practical activity make up the *method*.

No practical or scientific problem can be solved without a method. If, for example, we want to ascertain the chemical composition of a substance, we have to master the method of chemical analysis in the first place, i.e., to learn how to test this substance with appropriate chemical reagents, decompose it, determine the chemical properties of its constituents, etc. If we have to smelt a metal, we must learn the technology of smelting, i.e., to master the practical methods elaborated by people in the process of metallurgical production.

Specific methods are just as necessary in studying physical, biological and other phenomena. That explains why people devote so much time and effort to devising and mastering methods of practical and theoretical work.

A method is not a mechanical sum of different ways of research chosen by people at random without consideration for the phenomena being studied. The method itself is largely determined by the nature of these phenomena and their intrinsic laws. Hence each field of science or practical activity devises its own methods. The methods of physics, for example, differ from the methods of chemistry, the latter differ from the methods of biology, and so on.

By generalising the achievements of different sciences and mankind's practical activity, scientific philosophy has evolved its own method of knowledge—*materialist dialectics*. This method differs from the methods of concrete sciences in that it provides a key to understanding absolutely all fields of nature, society and thought, a key to understanding the world as a whole, and not only to understanding individual spheres of reality. The word "dialectics" is of ancient Greek origin. Initially it meant the ability to conduct disputes and bring out the truth by disclosing and resolving contradictions in the arguments of the opponents. Later it was applied as a method of cognising reality. Drawing on scientific achievements and society's practical experience at different stages of history, dialectics maintains that the world is an endless process of movement, regeneration, the demise of the old and the birth of the new. "For it (dialectical philosophy) nothing is absolute...," Engels wrote. "It reveals the transitory character of everything and in everything; nothing can endure before it except the uninterrupted process of becoming and passing away, of endless ascendancy from the lower to the higher."* Furthermore, dialectics views the internal contradictions inherent in objects and phenomena as the source of motion and development.

By explaining the process of development, the struggle of the new against the old and the inevitability of the victory of the new, dialectics helps progressive people to combat the obsolete social order and reactionary class forces. In our day dialectics is a powerful instrument in the hands of the working class and its Marxist parties for the cognition and revolutionary transformation of the world.

Metaphysics is a method which is the antithesis of materialist dialectics. The metaphysical approach to phenomena originated first in natural science, and in the 17th-18th centuries became current in philosophy, too. At the time metaphysics denied the development and the rise of the new, and understood motion as a simple displacement of bodies in space.

Since in our age of enormous social change and the scientific and technical revolution it is no longer possible to deny development as such, contemporary metaphysics has turned to misinterpreting the essence of development. Now it interprets development only as a qualitative increase or decrease, as simple repetition of what already exists, does not recognise the

---

* Friedrich Engels, *Ludwig Feuerbach and the End of Classical German Philosophy*, International Publishers, New York, 1941, p. 12.

emergence of the new, and negates internal contradictions as the source of development.

Contemporary metaphysics which does not recognise the progressive nature of development, the struggle between the new and the old and the inevitability of the victory of the new, expresses the interests of the reactionary forces which use it to fight against everything progressive. For example, it is employedd by the revisionists who renounce the class struggle, the socialist revolution and the dictatorship of the proletariat and preach social peace between the exploiters and the exploited and the idea of the peaceful development of capitalism into socialism. Metaphysics is also the theoretical basis of dogmatism, whose proponents turn a blind eye to the profound social changes taking place in the world and endeavour to solve vital contemporary problems without taking into account the continuously changing historical conditions.

Everyday life, science and practice prove the truth of dialectics. Its vitality is conclusively demonstrated by the contemporary development of society. The building and perfection of developed socialist society, the formation of a powerful world system of socialism and the steady growth of the forces of peace, democracy, national liberation and socialism convincingly attest to the triumph of the principles of Marxist dialectics.

Now that we have gained a general idea of materialism and dialectics we can define the subject matter of Marxist philosophy, i.e., dialectical and historical materialism.

3. The Subject Matter of Marxist Philosophy

When we define the subject matter of Marxist philosophy we ascertain the range of problems that it studies and see how it differs from other sciences.

The subject matter of philosophy changed constantly throughout the long centuries of its development. At first philosophy embraced all the knowledge that had been accumulated: knowledge of the world as a whole, of its individual objects and phenomena—the Earth, man, animals, minerals, etc. Then, as production developed and more and more knowledge was accumulated, mechanics, physics, chemistry, geology, history and other so-called concrete sciences separated from it one by one. And today there are scores of sciences which study the most diverse spheres of reality.

What does Marxist philosophy study?

The core of the subject matter of Marxist philosophy is the solution of the fundamental question of philosophy: the relation of consciousness to being. We already know that all philosophical systems must answer this question, but only Marxist philosophy has furnished a completely scientific, correct and consistent answer to it.

The philosophy of Marxism is *dialectical materialism*. It is *materialist* because in solving the fundamental question of philosophy it proceeds from the premise that matter, being, is primary and consciousness is secondary. It recognises the materiality and knowability of the world, and examines the world as it really is. Marxist philosophy is *dialectical* because it examines the material world in constant motion, development and regeneration.

On the basis of a correct solution of the fundamental question of philosophy, dialectical materialism discloses and studies *the more general laws* of the development of the material world.

We know that concrete sciences also study the laws of the development of the material world, but each is concerned with a definite area of reality: physics studies heat, electricity, magnetism and other physical phenomena; chemistry studies the chemical transformation of substances; biology studies the processes occurring in plants and animals, etc. The laws of these sciences define development only in the *given* sphere of reality and cannot explain its other fields. Take the laws of classical mechanics, for example. They merely disclose the essence of mechanical motion, i.e., simple displacement of bodies in space, and cannot explain chemical, biological or other processes. Although the laws of mechanics operate in all the above processes, they have no independent significance in them and are subordinated to other laws disclosing the essence of these processes (in chemical processes—the laws of chemistry, in biological processes—the laws of biology, etc.).

As distinct from the concrete sciences, dialectical materialism studies the *general laws* regulating all spheres of reality. Thus, all inorganic and organic objects, the phenomena of social life and consciousness develop on the basis of the law of unity and conflict of opposites, the law of the passage of quantitative into qualitative changes, and the law of negation of the negation. These laws of materialist dialectics will be examined in detail in other chapters.

Dialectical materialism also studies the laws governing the process of *cognition* which are a reflection of the laws of the objective world. By equipping man with a knowledge of the laws of nature, society and thought, dialectical materialism shows people how to cognise the world and also *how to bring about its revolutionary transformation*.

Consequently, dialectical materialism is a science which on the basis of a materialist solution of the fundamental question of philosophy discloses the more general, dialectical laws of the development of the material world and the ways for its cognition and revolutionary transformation.

There were philosophers prior to Marx who also endeavoured to discover the more general laws of development and give a complete picture of the world, and many of them achieved a certain measure of success. Yet they were unable to draw a true scientific picture of the world either owing to their idealistic views, or the narrowness of the metaphysical method. Their main drawback, however, was that they all stood aloof from the revolutionary struggle and the interests of the working people.

Marx and Engels, thanks to their active participation in the revolutionary struggle of the working class, their selfless service to the people and profound knowledge of the outstanding achievements of science and philosophy, were able to disclose these general laws and discover the dialectical-materialist essence of reality.

It is important to note that they discovered the dialectical-materialist nature of social development as well. They created *historical materialism,* the only existing scientific theory of social development, a method of the cognition and revolutionary transformation of society. Historical materialism is a *science which studies the more general laws of social development* and is a component part of Marxist-Leninist philosophy.

Marxist Philosophy and Other Sciences

The laws of dialectical materialism, as we now know, are of a general, universal nature. They operate everywhere: in inorganic nature, in living organisms, in man and in his thought. The universality of the laws of Marxist philosophy is of tremendous importance, because thanks to it they can be used to cognise the most diverse phenomena in the world. Hence the enormous significance of dialectical materialism for the development of other sciences. Having arisen in intimate association with the experience and progress of concrete sciences and being a generalisation of their conclusions, dialectical materialism promotes their development and equips them with a scientific method of study.

At the same time dialectical materialism by no means makes it unnecessary for man to master concrete sciences and assimilate mankind's scientific, social and historical experience. Since dialectical materialism emerged and is developing on the basis of scientific advances and practical experience it is essential to know these advances in order to master and correctly apply the laws of dialectical materialism.

Some contemporary non-Marxist philosophers (the so-called *positivists*) deny the importance of philosophy, of a scientific world outlook for the development of science and distort the essence of the interconnection of science and philosophy. As exponents of "positive" (applied) scientific knowledge they divorce philosophy from science and endeavour to prove that science needs no philosophy whatsoever, that "science is itself a philosophy".

The history of philosophy and science overturns these primitive views, and conclusively proves that the two are inseparable. The great Russian thinker Alexander Herzen compared philosophy with a mighty tree trunk, and science and its innumerable fields, with its branches. Just as there can be no tree without a trunk and branches, so science and philosophy are inconceivable one without the other. "Cut off the branches," he wrote, "and what remains is a dead log. Remove the trunk and the branches will wither away."

As it develops, natural science strengthens its links and interaction with philosophy. These links have become especially close in our day when natural scientists are solving such complicated problems as the character of elementary particles of matter, the origin of life, the development of cosmic bodies and many others. Profound philosophical generalisations are absolutely essential in our age of momentous scientific advances; the tremendous progress of natural science and the deep revolutionary changes that are taking place in it require the closest union of philosophy and science. In these circumstances, Lenin noted, a natural scientist must be a dialectical materialist.

Hence, it is not accidental that an increasing number of natural scientists in capitalist countries are turning into conscious adherents of Marxist philosophy. It helps them to find their bearings in the objective, material world and to reveal the dialectics of nature in their concrete scientific studies.

CHAPTER II

The Rise and Development of Marxist Philosophy

Marxist philosophy was evolved by the great leaders of the working class *Karl Marx* (1818-1883) and *Frederick Engels* (1820-1895). Is it merely the fruit of the brilliant minds of its founders, or is it the product of the epoch, a sign of the times? What causes had brought it into being?

The rise of Marxist philosophy was a natural result of historical development. It was brought about by concrete socio-economic conditions and had definite prerequisites in natural science and philosophy.

1. The Conditions and Prerequisites for the Rise of Marxist Philosophy

Socio-Economic Conditions

By mid-19th century, capitalism had replaced feudalism in many countries. Its advent promoted great progress in production and the rapid development of technology, science and culture.

At the same time capitalism created the proletariat, the class destined to destroy the capitalist system and carry out socialist transformations. Exploited by the bourgeoisie and deprived of elementary human rights, the proletariat began a bitter struggle against its enslavers. Under capitalism class contradictions became unusually acute and found their expression in numerous direct actions of the proletariat against the bourgeoisie. French workers rose in Lyons and Silesian weavers in Germany, and the Chartist movement in Britain gained in strength. The workers demanded better working conditions, higher wages, shorter working hours, etc. But in those days their actions were unorganised and spontaneous. They had a vague idea of the ultimate objectives for which they should fight and had no notion of effective ways and means of fighting against their class enemies. This created an urgent need for a scientific theory that would help the proletariat to learn the laws of social development, understand why the doom of capitalism was inevitable, and to become aware of its mission as the grave-digger of the bourgeoisie and the builder of a new, socialist system.

It follows that the very development of the proletarian movement confronted science with the immensely important task of evolving a revolutionary theory and forging an ideological weapon for the proletariat in its

16

struggle against capitalism and for socialism. And science in the person of its brilliant proponents Marx and Engels fulfilled this pressing demand of history: they created Marxism whose component part and theoretical foundation is Marxist philosophy—dialectical and historical materialism.

Prerequisites in Natural Science
and Theoretical Sources

The way for the emergence of Marxist philosophy was also paved by the entire progress of natural science and philosophical thought. The development of natural science was unusually rapid in the 19th century. It ceased to be a science which merely accumulated facts and studied individual objects and phenomena, and turned into a theoretical science concerned with explaining these facts and establishing the connections between them. Metaphysics in natural science gave way to dialectical ideas of the unity and historical development of the world.

The first breach in the metaphysical view of nature was made by the German philosopher *Immanuel Kant* (1724-1804) whose cosmogonic hypothesis proved that the Earth and the Solar system were not eternal, but came into being as a result of the long evolution of matter. Then geology, a science that deals with the history of the Earth's crust, came into being and physics, chemistry, biology and other sciences began to develop at a very rapid pace.

Three great discoveries of natural science played a particularly important role in shaping and substantiating dialectical materialist views on nature, namely, the discovery of the law of the conservation and transformation of energy, the theory of the cellular structure of living organisms and Darwin's theory of evolution.

The law of the conservation and transformation of energy discovered by the great Russian scientist *Mikhail Lomonosov*, the German scientist *Julius Robert von Mayer* and the English physicist *James Prescott Joule* convincingly demonstrates the material unity of the world, and the eternity and indestructibility of matter and motion. It also shows the great qualitative diversity of matter and motion and their variability and ability to pass from one form to another.

The theory of the cellular structure of the living tissue evolved by the Russian botanist *Pavel Goryaninov*, the Czech biologist *Jan Purkyne* and the German scientists *Matthias Jakob Schleiden* and *Theodor Schwann* showed that a material element, the cell, was the basis of any more or less complex organism. By demonstrating the cell's ability to change, they laid the groundwork for a correct understanding of the development of organisms.

With his theory of evolution the great English natural scientist *Charles Darwin,* as Lenin noted, overturned the view that the species of plants and animals were accidental, unconnected with anything, god-created and immutable. He scientifically proved that the complex, higher organisms had been formed from the simple, lower ones through the action of the laws of natural selection inherent in nature itself. Darwin also showed that man was a product of nature, a result of the prolonged evolution of living matter. This confirmed the basic idea of dialectics, namely the idea of development, of the transition from the lower to the higher, from the simple to the complex.

Alongside the achievements of natural science, the successes of philo-sophical thought in that period also played an enormous role in shaping a Marxist world outlook. As they evolved dialectical and historical materi-alism, Marx and Engels exhaustively studied the history of philosophy and used the best that philosophical thought acquired over the many centuries of its development. The direct theoretical source of Marxist philosophy was the 19th-century German classical philosophy, above all the philos-ophy of Hegel and Feuerbach.

Marx and Engels did not arrive at positions of dialectical materialism at once. In their youth they were attracted by the idealistic philosophy of *Georg Hegel* (1770-1831) which was widespread in Germany in their time. Hegel was an objective idealist. He believed that the world was created by the supra-human, objectively existing consciousness—Absolute Idea and World Spirit. Though the point of departure of his philosophical system was erroneous, he made a serious contribution to the development of philo-sophical thought by elaborating a harmonious system of *idealistic dialec-tics* as a totality of logical laws and categories.

Hegel evolved the basic laws of dialectics governing the development of ideas and thoughts. He showed that the development of ideas did not follow a closed circuit, but rose from lower to higher forms, that quantitative changes turned into qualitative ones in this process and that contradictions were the source of development. He characterised the basic concepts (cate-gories) of dialectics and disclosed their interconnection and ability to turn into each other. It was dialectics that Marx and Engels borrowed from Hegel's philosophy and which they interpreted from materialist positions and used to develop dialectical and historical materialism.

The materialism of *Ludwig Feuerbach* (1804-1872) powerfully influenced the formation of Marx's and Engels's world outlook. Feuerbach, who was a great materialist of his time, rejected idealism and religion and emphasised that philosophy should not be confined to thought alone and that it had to study nature and man. Nature, he maintained, existed outside of man, it was the first, primary and underived being. As regards man, he was a part of nature, a product of its long evolution. Consciousness, in Feuerbach's opinion, did not precede nature, but merely reflected and cognised it. Matter, nature, is cognisable and man can understand it by means of all his sensory organs.

The materialistic ideas in Feuerbach's philosophy helped Marx and Engels to discard Hegel's idealism and evolve dialectical and historical materialism. But as they used Feuerbach's philosophy, the founders of Marxism discerned its narrow limits and idealistic interpreting of social life; they were not satisfied with its contemplative nature and isolation from life and the people's struggle for liberation. They were firmly convinced that major philosophical and social problems had to be solved in the course of the revolutionary, political struggle and not in the solitude of studies.

Participation in the social and political struggle on the side of the working people and profound study of natural science, philosophy and history convinced Marx and Engels that idealism was insolvent and they resolutely moved from revolutionary democracy to the positions of scientific communism, of the proletariat. In the sphere of philosophy this meant that they created a qualitatively new philosophy—dialectical and historical materialism.

In evolving their philosophy Marx and Engels drew on Hegel's dialectics and Feuerbach's materialism which they critically revised, purged of all sorts of unscientific features and enriched with the vast experience of the revolutionary struggle of the proletariat and the latest scientific achievements.

By creating dialectical and historical materialism, Marx and Engels consummated a great revolution in philosophy.

2. The Essence of the Revolution in Philosophy Carried Out by Marxism

To ascertain the essence of this revolution means to establish what *new* features Marx and Engels introduced into philosophy and to perceive the new *qualitative* distinctions setting Marxist philosophy apart from the preceding philosophical systems.

What are the basic novel aspects of Marxist philosophy?

In the first place it differs from the past philosophical systems by its *class nature and the role it plays in social life*.

With every few exceptions pre-Marxist philosophers were in the service of the exploiters and consequently did not set themselves the goal of remaking the world to suit the interests of the working people.

Marxist philosophy is another thing. It does not serve a handful of exploiters, but expresses the interests of the proletariat, the most advanced class, the interests of multi-million masses which are the real makers of history. Marx and Engels not only founded the new philosophy but were also the *leaders of the developing movement of the proletariat*. It was they who showed that the only road to the liberation of the working people lay through socialist revolution and the dictatorship of the proletariat. They wholly dedicated their brilliant minds, enormous creative energies and outstanding talent for organisation to the lofty cause of emancipating the working people from exploitation, to the cause of socialism.

Having aligned themselves with the oppressed class, the proletariat, Marx and Engels created a philosophy which became its spiritual weapon in the struggle against capitalism and a powerful means of remaking life. This basically altered and tremendously increased the role of philosophy in social development. It gripped the minds of the masses and turned into a great material force. Describing this crucial feature of dialectical and historical materialism Marx wrote: "The philosophers have only *interpreted* the world in various ways; the point, however, is to *change* it."* Marxist philosophy owes its strength to its organic bonds with life, to the fact that it serves the struggle waged by the working class against capitalism, for socialism and communism.

The most important manifestation of the revolution which Marxism brought in philosophy is the *attainment of organic unity of materialism and dialectics*.

We have learned from the history of philosophy that dialectics and materialism originated long before Marxism. But the fault of the old philosophy was that materialism and dialectics in it were often separated from each other. Hegel was a dialectician, but not a materialist, while Feuerbach was a materialist, but not a dialectician. Only Marx and Engels bridged the gap between materialism and dialectics and united them into an integral dialectical-materialist world outlook. This is one of the most important

---

* Karl Marx, "Theses on Feuerbach", in: Karl Marx, Frederick Engels, *Collected Works*, Vol. 5, Moscow, 1976, p. 8.

aspects of Marxist philosophy making it qualitatively different from the preceding philosophies.

The rise of Marxism also signified a *revolution in the views on society*. Pre-Marxist philosophers idealistically interpreted social development, in the belief that it was motivated only by the ideas of people, by their consciousness. Marx and Engels contrasted this idealistic view with a materialistic interpretation of history. They were the first to raise and correctly solve the fundamental question of philosophy, the relation of consciousness to being as applied to society. They incontrovertibly proved that it was not the social consciousness of the people that determined their being, but, on the contrary, the social being and, above all, the production of material values, that determined social consciousness and that social development depended on material causes and not on people's ideas, wishes or intentions. As a result, the history of society came to be understood as a law-governed, natural process of the replacement of the lower modes of production by higher ones, and not as a chaotic conglomeration of phenomena. It was proved that this replacement was not spontaneous but followed objective laws which are independent of man's will and consciousness.

The Partisanship of Marxist Philosophy

Bourgeois philosophers often claim that their philosophy is non-partisan and expresses the interests of all peoples regardless of their class affiliations. But why is it that their conceptions are always on the side of the capitalists, defend private property and justify exploitation and war? It turns out that the assertions of bourgeois philosophers that they are independent of classes and parties are not true and that they use the mask of "non-partisanship" to conceal the class, partisan nature of their philosophy and its utter dedication to the rich.

As distinct from the bourgeois ideologists who hide the class nature of their conceptions, the founders of Marxism-Leninism openly proclaimed the principle of partisanship in philosophy. This principle characterises philosophy's inviolable connection with politics and the interests of definite social classes and parties. Since philosophy is a product of a definite epoch and classes, it always reflects the demands of that epoch and upholds the interests of those classes. Partisanship in philosophy does in fact consist of service to definite classes.

Marxist philosophy arose as the spiritual weapon of the working class in its struggle against the bourgeoisie. Its proletarian party spirit consists above all in its selfless dedication to the working class, to the working people, and irreconcilability towards the policy of the reactionary bourgeoisie. The principle of partisanship in philosophy demands, as Lenin wrote, "to pursue your *own* line and to combat the *whole line* of the forces and classes hostile to us".*

Partisanship in philosophy is displayed by the adoption of a definite stand in the struggle between materialism and idealism which has been in progress for more than two millennia already. Far from abating, this struggle has intensified many times over in the present epoch and finds its expression in the struggle between the scientific world outlook and the idealistic world outlook of the reactionary bourgeoisie. Partisanship in Marxist philosophy means firm adherence in this struggle to consistent materialist positions, defence and development of dialectical and historical materialism and determined resistance against any ideology that is hostile to Marxism. This demand has become particularly urgent in our day when a bitter struggle between the two ideologies—socialist and bourgeois—is going on in the world, and when the bourgeoisie resorts to the most refined forms of idealism against Marxist philosophy. Integrity and vigilance in ideological issues have never been more important than they are today.

Following in the wake of bourgeois ideologists, modern revisionists distort the Marxist-Leninist principle of partisanship in philosophy and allege that partisanship and scientific objectivity are incompatible. They even say that bourgeois ideology is above-class and, therefore, the only scientific philosophy in the world. They demand an end to the struggle against this ideology because it allegedly embraces general human knowledge which is beneficial and necessary to all social classes.

In reality, however, the bourgeoisie continuously falsifies the laws of social development in the hope of perpetuating capitalism which history has doomed to extinction. As regards the proletariat, it is remaking the world and therefore has to know the real laws. It is all for science because a scientific world outlook is the only reliable guide to action.

The proletariat's ultimate goal is the victory of communism. At the same time the movement towards communism is the objective content of contemporary social development. It follows then that the objective course of history and the class interests of the proletariat fully coincide. That is why the *coincidence between the consistent defence of the proletariat's interests and scientific objectivity is a key feature of partisanship in Marxist-Leninist philosophy.*

---

* V. I. Lenin, "Materialism and Empirio-Criticism", *Collected Works*, Vol. 14, p. 343.

3. The Creative Nature of Marxist-Leninist Philosophy

Marxist philosophy is a *creative, developing* science and not a parcel of immutable, petrified principles taken on trust. It does not stand still, but moves forward keeping abreast of the continuously changing life and is daily enriched by the latest achievements in society's historical development and in natural science.

Marxist philosophy arose at a time when capitalism was ascending and social development was relatively slow and tranquil. The historical situation changed radically at the turn of the 20th century. Capitalism passed into its last, imperialist, stage, and economic and political contradictions became particularly acute. The period of relatively peaceful development ended with the advent of imperialism and gave way to social storms and revolutions.

This period, characterised by a radical break-up of social relations, coincided in time with a revolution in natural science. The discovery of the electron, radioactivity and other major scientific achievements overturned the old conceptions of matter and its properties that metaphysics had regarded as final and immutable.

Obviously, these new conditions necessitated the creative development of Marxist philosophy. It was imperative to generalise the newly-acquired experience of the proletariat's revolutionary struggle and the latest achievements of natural science, all the more so because the forces hostile to Marxism became more active and intensified their attacks on dialectical and historical materialism, the theoretical foundation of the working class's world outlook.

At the end of the 19th century the centre of the international working-class movement began to shift to Russia where the first bourgeois-democratic revolution of the epoch of imperialism with the proletariat as its leader was maturing, and objective prerequisites for its development into a socialist revolution were taking shape. Russia became the birthplace of Leninism. *Leninism is Marxism of the new historical epoch, the epoch of imperialism and proletarian revolutions, the epoch of the transition from capitalism to socialism and the building of communist society.* Therefore, it is not accidental that the further creative development of Marxist philosophy is indissolubly bound up with the name of the leader of the Russian and international proletariat, *Vladimir Lenin* (1870-1924). His contribution to Marxist philosophy is so great and multifarious that it constitutes a stage, an epoch in the history of philosophical thought.

The Leninist Stage in the Development of Philosophy

The Leninist stage in the development of philosophy covers a period from the end of the 19th century to the present day.

Lenin made a great contribution to philosophy by upholding and further developing dialectical and historical materialism in the new historical conditions. His theoretical work was directly connected with the revolutionary struggle of the proletariat and socialist construction in the USSR. He not only enriched Marxist philosophy but applied its principles in practice. Lenin founded the Communist Party, a party of a new, revolutionary type, under whose leadership Russia's workers and peasants destroyed capitalism and built the world's first socialist state. He drew up the plan for socialist and communist construction and to his last days stood at the head of the people and the party which are translating this plan into reality.

In the new historical epoch it was up to the working class and its Marxist party to transform society along revolutionary lines, destroy capitalism and build socialism. Consequently, Lenin devoted special attention to analysing the patterns of social development, and above all, to ascertaining the essence of capitalism and determining the ways of establishing and consolidating the new society. Taking account of the changed historical conditions, he further developed the Marxist theory of socialist revolution and produced arguments proving that socialism could be built first in several or even in one country. His theory of socialist revolution had an enormous impact on the course of social development.

Lenin also enriched the Marxist teaching on classes and the class struggle, the dictatorship of the proletariat and its forms, the role played by the masses in history, the role played by the party of the working class, by progressive ideas, etc.

He made a major contribution to the elaboration of problems of dialectics. In the struggle against metaphysicians of all hues he upheld and further developed the Marxist theory of the laws and categories of materialist dialectics, devoting particular attention to the nucleus of dialectics—the law of unity and the conflict of opposites.

Lenin evolved the dialectical-materialist theory of knowledge. He searchingly analysed the crisis which occurred in natural science at the turn of the century as a result of scientific discoveries and showed that only materialist dialectics could resolve it.

He fought consistently against bourgeois ideology, revisionism and dogmatism. By exposing the essential features of revisionism and dogmatism and the trends of their development, he armed the Marxists for the struggle against revisionists and dogmatists.

Lenin's contribution to Marxist philosophy will be examined in greater detail in the ensuing chapters.

After Lenin, the philosophy of Marxism has been developed by his associates and pupils, prominent leaders of the Communist Party of the Soviet Union and the fraternal communist and workers' parties.

Marxist-Leninist philosophy has been further developed in the decisions of Congresses, Conferences and Central Committee Plenary Meetings of the CPSU and other Marxist parties and in the resolutions of international meetings of Communists. By developing Marxist philosophy these documents attest to the correct application of its propositions and conclusions in analysing the historical situation, in the revolutionary struggle and in socialist and communist construction. The creative development of the scientific theory of Marxism-Leninism, Marxist-Leninist philosophy, its organic combination with the revolutionary struggle of the working people, and with socialist and communist construction are the most powerful and the most notable aspect of the entire historical activity of the CPSU. The Party bases its whole revolutionary activity on the sound foundation of Marxist-Leninist theory. As it develops Marxist theory, the CPSU conducts an offensive against the ideology of anti-communism and various bourgeois and revisionist conceptions.

Marxist-Leninist philosophy develops in a bitter struggle chiefly against reactionary bourgeois ideology. The age-long history of philosophy has not put an end to the division of philosophers into two opposing camps—materialists and idealists. And today the battle between these two trends is a reflection of the struggle between progressive and reactionary classes.

Being the world outlook of the revolutionary proletariat and all the working people, Marxist-Leninist materialist philosophy is a formidable weapon in the struggle against imperialist reaction, for socialism and progress. It is opposed by the idealist philosophy of the reactionary, moribund imperialist bourgeoisie. This philosophy plays a reactionary role because it endeavours to save the capitalist system, keep millions of workers in the grip of idealism, refute Marxism-Leninism and prevent the ideas of materialism and dialectics from influencing broad sections of the people.

There are many trends and schools in contemporary bourgeois philosophy, but the distinctions between them are inessential. In the main thing—their idealist substance, anti-Marxist trend and service to imperialist reaction—they are all alike. Some of these trends overtly advocate idealism, mysticism and hatred for science. Others do this in a more refined way; they try to use the latest achievements of science for this purpose and to adapt themselves to the requirements of social development. Still others openly revive medieval scholasticism and glorify religious dogmas.

But try as they might the ideologists of contemporary imperialist bourgeoisie will neither disprove Marxist-Leninist theory, nor stem the growth of its influence. More and more convincingly history demonstrates the triumph of Marxism-Leninism and its materialist philosophy.

DIALECTICAL MATERIALISM

CHAPTER III

Matter and the Forms of Its Existence

We already know that the main thing in the subject matter of dialectical materialism is the solution of the fundamental question of philosophy—the relation of matter to consciousness. Let us now analyse in detail *what is matter and what are the forms of its existence.*

1. What Is Matter

Man is surrounded by an infinite number of the most diverse bodies. These include both bodies of inorganic nature—from infinitesimal particles of the atom to huge cosmic bodies, and living organisms—from the simplest to the most complex. Some are next to us: we live amidst them and constantly feel their presence, while others are removed from us by extremely great distances. Some we see with the naked eye, but to observe others we have to use the most sophisticated instruments and equipment. These bodies possess the most diverse properties, qualities and features.

Amazed by the diversity of the world, man long ago pondered the possibility of all the surrounding bodies stemming from a single basis and having similar features.

Gradually, man's practical activities and the development of science have convinced him that however much objects and phenomena differ, however diverse their properties, they are all material and exist outside and independent of his consciousness. Natural sciences have indisputably proved that the Earth had existed many millions of years before man and living organisms in general appeared on it. This signifies that matter, nature, is objective and independent of man and his consciousness, and that consciousness itself is merely a product of the long evolution of the material world.

The philosophical concept, or category, of matter expresses the general property of objects and phenomena, which consists in their being objective reality, existing outside of man's consciousness and reflected in his consciousness.

Recognition of the objectivity of the world around us and recognition of the ability of the human mind to cognise this world constitute the basic principles of the dialectical-materialist world outlook. This means that the concept of matter, reflecting these cardinal principles, is the most important, pivotal category of dialectical materialism.

The category of matter is an extremely broad concept, encompassing not a separate object or process, not a group of objects and phenomena, but *all* of objective reality. Abstracting itself from the given distinctions, properties and sides of separate objects, from their concrete connections and interaction, this concept expresses the *common, main thing* in all these objects, namely, *objectivity*, i.e., their existence independent of man's consciousness. The concept of matter not only gives an idea of the general properties of the objective world as such; it is also a *primary category of knowledge*. Pointing to man's ability to cognise the world and indicating the source of our knowledge, it also provides the basis for solving major problems of the theory of knowledge of dialectical materialism.

The concept of matter is also of great importance for the other sciences, particularly natural science. Any science would be reduced to a meaningless exercise of the human mind if it did not study one or another aspect of objective reality.

A truly scientific, all-embracing definition of matter was given by Lenin in his book *Materialism and Empirio-Criticism*. "Matter is a philosophical category," he wrote, "denoting the objective reality which is given to man by his sensations, and which is copied, photographed and reflected by our sensations, while existing independently of them."*

It is difficult to overestimate the significance of Lenin's definition of matter. Summing up mankind's experience over the centuries, it gives people a correct understanding of the world around them, teaches them to proceed in their practical work and theoretical studies from reality itself, from the objective material conditions and not from arbitrary, subjective ideas. Asserting that the world is knowable, it opens up boundless vistas to human reason, stimulates the mind and helps man penetrate the deepest secrets of the world.

Lenin's definition of matter reflects the fundamental contrast of materialism to idealism and agnosticism. It also has a deep atheistic meaning. Indeed, if matter is primary and eternal, it is uncreatable and indestructible, it is the inner final cause of everything existing. In a world where matter is the primary cause, the primary foundation of everything, there is room neither for God nor any other supernatural forces.

---

* V. I. Lenin, "Materialism and Empirio-Criticism", *Collected Works*, Vol. 14, p. 130.

That is why idealists and the clergy have always bitterly fought against recognition of matter. Idealists of the past, from Plato to Berkeley, engaged in "destroying" the concept of matter, while Machists* even launched a crusade against it. Today there are numerous idealists and revisionists who continue the battle. The purpose of the attacks on the concept of matter has been to undermine the fundamental concept of materialism, to drive matter out of philosophy and science, and thereby clear the way for idealism, agnosticism and religion.

These attacks, however, are absolutely pointless. Scientific progress and all man's practical experience conclusively prove that matter does exist as objective reality and that it is infinite and eternal. All things, objects and processes are merely manifestations or forms of matter in motion. That is why the world around us is a *single material world.* But the forms of matter, as we can see from personal experience and scientific discoveries, are diverse. This signifies that the material world is a *unity* of *diversity.* In the material world there is not a single thing, however minute, which can arise out of nothing or disappear without trace. The destruction of one thing gives rise to another and this to a third, and so on *ad infinitum.* Concrete things change, they are transformed one into another, but matter neither disappears nor is created anew in the process.

The Concept of Matter and the Picture of the World Given by Natural Science

The philosophical concept of matter must be distinguished from the *picture of the world given by natural science,* from the views on the structure, state and properties of *concrete* forms of matter which are elaborated by natural science in the course of its development. These views constantly change, develop and at times undergo a radical transformation. This, however, does not affect the truth of the philosophical understanding of matter as objective reality existing independent of our consciousness.

In an effort to refute materialism, idealists deliberately confuse the philosophical concept of matter with the views of natural science on the structure of concrete material bodies. A change in these views, renunciation of old ideas and their replacement by new, more exact and improved ideas, is

---

* Machists were proponents of an idealist trend in philosophy at the end of the 19th and beginning of the 20th centuries named after the Austrian philosopher Ernst Mach. Lenin gave a profound and comprehensive critique of Machism in his *Materialism and Empirio-Criticism* published in 1909.

held up by them as the "disappearance" of matter, as the "collapse" of materialism.

For many centuries, for example, many materialists metaphysically identified matter with the atom, which they regarded as impenetrable and indivisible. But at the end of the 19th century, scientists discovered the electron, a minute integral part of the atom, and then other particles. As a result, the atom, which for centuries had been regarded as the ultimate, indivisible unit of the world, proved to be an extremely complex phenomenon. The properties of the electron, it was discovered, were entirely unlike the formerly accepted conceptions of the properties of the atom. This confused metaphysically thinking physicists, while idealist philosophers, who took advantage of the ensuing difficulties, gained a pretext for speaking about the "dematerialisation" of the atom and the "disappearance" of matter.

In *Materialism and Empirio-Criticism* Lenin proved the untenability of these assertions. He showed that the latest discoveries of natural science do not result in the disappearance of matter, but only of obsolete knowledge of it. Yesterday the limit of our knowledge was the atom; today it is the electron, while tomorrow this limit too will disappear. Our knowledge reaches deep into matter, revealing more and more of its properties, its ever deeper and finer formations. The electron which was discovered in its time is precisely such form of matter. Lenin, referring to the latest achievements of science, concluded that "the electron is as *inexhaustible* as the atom, nature is infinite".*

Lenin's ideas of the qualitative diversity of matter and the inexhaustible diversity of its structure and properties have been fully corroborated by the findings of contemporary science, and of physics in particular.

Substance is a form of matter known in modern physics. Everything that has a mechanical mass or, as physicists say, a rest mass, is a substance. All visible or, as they are also called, macroscopic bodies that surround man are substantive. These bodies consist of molecules which in turn contain atoms. Bodies, molecules and atoms are exceptionally diverse. This, however, does not exhaust the qualitative diversity of substance. The atoms themselves have a very intricate structure, consisting of so-called elementary particles—protons and neutrons, which make up the nucleus of the atom, and electrons that revolve around the nucleus at a tremendous speed. The enumerated particles and also other "elementary" particles known to science (mesons, hyperons, neutrinos, etc.) are the smallest particles of

---

* V. I. Lenin, "Materialism and Empirio-Criticism", *Collected Works*, Vol. 14, p. 262.

substance known today. They are called elementary, because so far scientists have not succceded in splitting them into smaller material formations. There is no doubt, however, that they too, like the atom, have an intricate structure. It is worth noting that elementary particles exist not only as part of atoms and nuclei, but also in a free state. Many of these particles, for example, are contained in cosmic radiation.

In recent years, antiparticles (positrons, antiprotons and others) have been discovered; they differ from the corresponding particles of substance (electron, proton) by their opposite electrical charge.

When Lenin wrote *Materialism and Empirio-Criticism* only one elementary particle was known, the electron. Today there are dozens of elementary particles and antiparticles known to science. Physicists have discovered not only numerous particles of the atom but, by establishing their diverse properties, have also demonstrated that these particles, like the atom, are inexhaustible. Today the electron can no longer be conceived as some kind of an unchanging tiny sphere. It possesses properties of discontinuity and continuity, or properties of both a particle and a wave, and also a mass, an electrical charge, a magnetic moment, etc. Other elementary particles, too, possess a wide range of properties.

Substance exists in a variety of states. In our everyday life we usually deal with *solid, liquid* or *gaseous* substances. And yet the most widespread state of substance in the world is *plasma*, a gaseous condition created by electrically charged particles—electrons and ions. Stars, nebulae, interstellar gas are in a state of plasma, while solid, liquid and gaseous bodies, which are so widespread on the Earth, are, on the whole, a great rarity in the Universe.

Plasma resembles gas, but it has different properties: under the influcnce of a powerful magnetic field the movement of its particles acquires a specific, so-called spiral character. The magnetic field acts as the walls of a vessel capable of retaining plasma in a set condition and volume. In view of these properties plasma is also regarded as yet another, fourth form of matter.

Today scientists devote especially great attention to plasma. Its study creates infinite opportunities for technical progress; in particular, it opens the way for controlling thermonuclear reactions and thus obtaining a practically inexhaustible source of energy.

If an ordinary solid substance is compressed to an exceptionally great density, the electrons of its atoms penetrate the atomic nucleus and by uniting with its protons turn into neutrons. This creates another, *neutron* condition of substance. The distinguishing properties of a substance in a neutron form is its enormous (tens of thousands of times greater than in metals which are the best conductors) electric conductivity, the appearance of powerful magnetic fields when electricity passes through it, and amazing, unparalleled density. Suffice it to say that just one cubic centimetre of a substance in its neutron state weighs not less than a million tons.

The *field* is another basic form of matter known to modern science. The physical field is a material formation which interconnects bodies and transmits action from one body to another. The gravitational field (gravity) and the electromagnetic field (light is one of its varieties) were known already in the 19th century. Photons are particles of the electromagnetic field, which differ from particles of substance in that they have no rest mass characteristic of the latter. Moreover, in a vacuum photons always travel at a constant velocity of 300,000 kilometres per second, whereas the velocity of particles of substance can vary greatly, but cannot be higher than that of photons.

In addition to the gravitational and electromagnetic fields there are also the nuclear, meson and electron-positron fields. Corresponding to each field are definite particles, whose properties are not identical with the properties of photons.

Thus, both substance and field are diverse and inexhaustible in their structure and properties.

The boundaries between substance and field are distinct only in the macroscopic, visible world. In the sphere of micro-processes, however, these boundaries are relative. Some particles of substance (for example, mesons) are at the same time also particles (quanta) of the corresponding field. Substance and field are inextricably connected; they interact and under certain circumstances are capable of being transformed one into another. In certain conditions two particles of substance (electron and positron) can be transformed into photons, particles of the electromagnetic field. The practical realisation of this experiment was one of the greatest achievements of physics, which once again demonstrated the material unity of the world, its changeability and mobility.

Studies of the particles larger than molecules, known as polymeric chemical compounds (rubber, proteins, cellulose, starch and others), have provided an important contribution to the theory of the structure of matter. The main distinction of these compounds is that they are formed through numerous repetitions of similar groups of atoms bound into chains or other more complex formations.

By the discovery of polymers, the human mind penetrated a field which really lies on the boundary between the micro- and the macro-world. Since many of the polymeric compounds, particularly proteins, serve as material for the formation of living substance, their successful study is an important step in ascertaining the essence of the phenomena of life, in mastering and controlling vital processes.

All the achievements of modern physics, chemistry and other sciences thus confirm the theses of dialectical materialism concerning the objectivity of matter, the unity and diversity of the world, the infinity of matter and boundlessness of human knowledge. It should be noted, however, that each science, notwithstanding its great achievements, also has its difficulties and unsolved problems which are used by the enemies of materialism in order to discredit it.

For instance, some bourgeois philosophers and idealistically minded physicists take advantage of the fact that elementary particles cannot be directly observed and say that they are logical (reasoned) substances and not material bodies.

Actually, however, the atomic particles are just as material and objective as the atom itself, as the molecules formed from atoms and the bodies formed from molecules. All of them are only elements of one nature, the material world. If the atom and the particles comprising it did not exist, then the atomic power stations, the first of which was built by the Soviet people, would not have functioned, and the atomic icebreakers, the first of which bears the name of great Lenin, would not have sailed the seas.

And so our knowledge about the structure and properties of definite material formations, whether electron, atom, molecule or any other body, is relative, and subject to change. It changed in the past and will change again in the future. But for all that matter remains an objective reality. It is the categorical, unqualified recognition of the existence of matter outside man's consciousness and sensations that sets dialectical materialism apart from all forms of idealism, including agnosticism.

The world by its nature, as we have seen, is material: all that exists represents various forms and kinds of matter. But matter is not something inert and stagnant. It constantly moves in time and space. Motion, space and time are the basic forms of being of matter. For a deeper understanding of the material essence of the world we have to examine these forms. We shall begin with motion.

2. Motion—a Form of Existence of Matter

The universal character of the motion of matter was recognised by pre-Marxist materialists, but they interpreted it in a narrow, metaphysical way. They did not associate motion with change, development of bodies, and often conceived it only as mechanical displacement in space.

Dialectical materialism does not reduce the diversity of forms of motion to a single mechanical or any other form, but associates motion with change, development of bodies, the coming into being of the new and the passing away of the old. Motion is understood by dialectical materialism as any change, as *change in general* which encompasses all the processes transpiring in the Universe—from the simplest mechanical displacement to such an extremely complex process as human thinking.

Matter exists only in motion, through which it manifests or reveals itself. The facts of daily life, the development of science and practice have given convincing proof of this.

Let us take, for example, the atom. It exists as a definite material body only in so far as the elementary particles forming it are in constant motion. Outside of the motion of these particles the atom could not exist, nor could there be any other body without motion. As soon as metabolic interchange between the organism and the environment ceases (this is also a form of motion), the living organism perishes.

Due to motion material bodies manifest themselves, act on our sense organs. The Sun, for example, constantly irradiates countless moving particles into cosmic space. When they reach the Earth, these particles act on our sense organs and make the existence of the Sun known to us. If it were not for the movement of these particles we would not even suspect the Sun's existence; after all, the Sun is about 150 million kilometres away from the Earth.

Similarly, all other material bodies exist, manifest themselves only in motion. Not only elementary particles in atoms are in motion, but also the atoms in molecules and the molecules in bodies. The whole vast mass of terrestrial and cosmic bodies is in motion. Likewise, living organisms and social life undergo changes. It is impossible to find a single particle of the material world which does not move or change.

Motion is thus a form of the existence of matter, its inalienable attribute. *"Motion is the mode of existence of matter.* Never anywhere has there been matter, without motion, nor can there be,"* Engels wrote.

Motion Is Absolute. Rest Is Relative

The motion of matter is *absolute* and *eternal*, it can neither be created nor destroyed, inasmuch as matter itself is uncreatable and indestructible. The law of conservation and transformation of energy is the proof

* Frederick Engels, *Anti-Dühring*, Moscow, 1977, p. 77.

furnished by natural science that motion is uncreatable and indestructible. This law states that, like matter, motion does not disappear and does not arise anew, but is merely modified, is converted from one form into another.

But if motion is eternal, absolute, can we speak of rest?

Of course we can and must speak of it. In the course of material changes there are also moments of equilibrium, of rest. But they affect only particular objects and processes and not matter in its entirety. The absoluteness of motion necessarily presupposes rest as well, the latter being an indispensable prerequisite for the development of the world. An object arises in motion, while rest fixes, as it were, the result of motion, in consequence of which this object is preserved for a certain time and remains what it is.

In contrast to the absoluteness of motion, rest is *relative* and must not be understood as some kind of a dead, inert state. A body can be at rest only in relation to some other body, but it necessarily takes part in the general motion of matter. The house in which we live is in a state of rest in relation to the Earth's surface, but together with the Earth, it revolves around the Earth's axis, around the Sun, etc. Moreover, even when a body is in a state of rest, physical, chemical or other processes take place in it all the time.

The motion of matter is eternal, absolute, while rest is temporary, relative: it is only a moment of motion.

Forms of Motion of Matter

There are many kinds and forms of motion. Drawing on the achievements of natural science, dialectical materialism classifies the kinds of motion, singling out from their diversity the *basic* forms. Engels gave the first scientific classification of the forms of motion of matter. In the basic forms he included: mechanical, physical, chemical, biological and social; moreover, he associated each one with a definite form of matter— mechanical, with celestial and terrestrial bodies; physical, with molecules, etc.

Engels' classification of the main forms of motion still retains its scientific value, but the latest achievements of science have substantially enriched our knowledge of these forms.

In the 19th century *mechanical motion*, for example, was chiefly understood as the displacement of macroscopic bodies in space. Now, however, it has been established that spatial displacement is inherent in all material formations, from elementary particles to a living organism. Mechanical motion must not be associated only with one form of matter, macroscopic, that is, visible bodies. This motion is inherent in any kind of matter, in any other form of motion, although in other, non-mechanical forms, it is of a subordinate, auxiliary character.

Our ideas concerning the *physical form* of motion of matter have been substantially enriched, above all due to the profound penetration of physics into the atom. Scientists have discovered and studied such hitherto unknown kinds of physical motion as intra-atomic and intra-nuclear motion. Engels associated the physical form of motion chiefly with molecular processes. In the light of contemporary data, however, this form of motion embraces thermal, electrical, magnetic, intra-atomic and intra-nuclear processes as well as numerous other processes occurring in solid, liquid and gaseous bodies due to the movement of elementary particles.

The *chemical form* of motion of matter is connected with the combination or separation of atoms, with the resultant formation or break-up of molecules, of which all chemical compounds consist. Chemical processes are accompanied by the motion of electrons forming the outer shell of atoms. Chemical transmutations are widespread in both inorganic and organic nature.

Biological motion is one of the most complex forms of motion of matter, encompassing all the diverse processes occurring in living organisms. These processes are associated with protein bodies, the carriers of life, which maintain continuous metabolic change with their environment. This metabolism results in a constant self-regeneration of the chemical composition of the protein bodies, which is the chief characteristic of any living thing.

Social life, the history of human society, is an even higher form of motion of matter, which differs essentially and qualitatively from all the preceding ones. It appeared with the rise of human society and its major distinction is the process of material production, determining all other aspects of social life.

The forms of motion of matter are *interconnected and inseparable*. Their unity and interconnection is based on the material unity of the world. One form of motion, given appropriate conditions, can turn into another. Mechanical motion, for example, may cause heat, sound, light, electricity and other kinds of physical motion. The interaction of physical processes leads to chemical transformations, while chemical processes in certain conditions give rise to organic life.

The lower forms are necessarily included in the higher form of motion of matter. For example, biological motion is connected with definite mechanical, physical and chemical processes. But higher forms of motion cannot be reduced to lower ones. The higher form of motion possesses its own particular laws, which distinguish it from the lower and determine its qualitative specific features. Thus, the laws of metabolism set organic life apart from inorganic nature. The mechanical, physical and chemical processes inherent in organisms have no independent significance and are subordinated to the chief process in the organism—metabolism.

Recognition of the absolute and universal character of motion, with necessary account of the qualitative distinction of each form, the ability of these forms to become mutually transformed, and the impossibility of reducing the higher forms to lower ones—this is the essence of the dialectical-materialist concept of motion.

Matter Cannot Be Divorced from Motion

We have stated earlier that there can be no inert, immobile state of matter, that matter and motion are inseparable. Yet even today some people think of matter as such without motion, divorcing matter from motion.

Such, for example, are the proponents of the so-called theory of the heat death of the Universe who, distorting the findings of science, predict the coming "end" of the world, the "death" of everything existing. They proceed from the fact, long ago established by science, that all forms of energy are easily converted into thermal energy, while the reverse process is more complex and demands an additional expenditure of energy. It is also true that any heated body placed in an environment with a lower temperature cools, transferring its heat to it.

Applying these principles to the entire Universe, these theorists arrive at the conclusion that, in time, fiery celestial bodies will transfer all their heat to cold cosmic space. That being the case, the Universe, in their opinion, will ultimately reach a state of "heat balance" or "heat death", turning into a monstrous conglomeration of frozen bodies, while all forms of motion of matter will become thermal energy incapable of further conversion, and matter will lose the ability to move. Although this theory was criticised and refuted by Engels,* idealists and theologians continue to defend it and use it as "proof" that the "end" of the world is inevitable.

Scientifically, the theory of the heat death of the Universe is completely unfounded and ignores the law of conservation and transformation of energy which asserts the indestructibility of motion not only quantitatively but also qualitatively. According to this law, motion cannot exist in only one form, nor can matter exist in a state of immobility, i.e., a state in which motion would no longer pass from one form into another. The transforma-

---

* See Frederick Engels, *Dialectics of Nature,* Moscow, 1974, pp. 38-39.

tion of forms of motion is as natural and law-governed as the quantitative conservation of motion during these transformations.

The latest discoveries of astronomy show that the cycle of matter in the Universe does not cease for a single moment. In some regions of cosmic space, matter and energy are dispersed; in others they are re-concentrated, giving rise to new celestial bodies. Soviet scientists have established that new stars are still being formed, and not merely single stars but entire groups (associations) of stars. This proves that there can be no immobile state of matter.

But then, perhaps, motion exists by itself, without any material carrier?

This is precisely what the advocates of *energetism*, a trend in philosophy and natural science which arose at the turn of the century, think. They reduce matter to motion and energy. This is nothing more than a refusal to recognise matter and is idealism pure and simple.

Present-day champions of energetism are particularly vociferous in their idealist views. Falsifying the latest achievements of science, they speak of the "annihilation" of matter, its conversion into "pure" energy. To this end, for example, they idealistically interpret the conversion of a pair of elementary particles of substance (electron and positron) into photons, particles of the electromagnetic field (light). By regarding light as "pure" energy, energy without matter, and substance as the only form of matter, adherents of energetism have arrived at the absolutely erroneous conclusion that in this instance matter disappears and is converted into energy. The photon, however, is a particle of the field, a special form of matter. The conversion of the electron and positron into photons is not transformation of matter into energy, but conversion of one kind of matter— substance, into another—the field.

The complete bankruptcy of energetism is disclosed by the advances of modern physics and above all by the law of the interconnection of mass and energy discovered early in this century. According to this law, the mass of a body is always connected with a corresponding quantity of energy. It is difficult to establish this dependence at relatively small speeds, but when a body travels at a velocity close to that of light (and elementary particles possess such velocities during nuclear transformations), the increase of its mass becomes noticeable. That the mass changes depending on velocity has been confirmed experimentally. Mass, however, is a measure of matter, while energy is a measure of motion. Consequently, the given law reveals the direct connection between the unity of matter and motion.

It follows from the above that there is neither matter without motion nor "pure" motion divorced from matter, nor could there be any. Matter and motion are inseparable.

3. Space and Time

The Philosophical Concept of Space and Time

When we look closely at the objects around us we find that each one is not only in motion, but also possesses extension, or size. Objects may be big or small, but they all have length, width and height, occupy a definite place, and have a volume. Objects in nature possess not only extension, but are also located in a certain way in relation to each other. Some of them are located farther away from us or nearer to us than others, higher or lower, to the right or to the left.

The philosophical concept of *space* reflects the universal property of material bodies to possess extension, to occupy a definite place and to be located in a particular way among other objects of the world.

Objects not only exist in space, but also follow each other in a definite sequence. The place of some objects is taken by others, which in turn are replaced by still others and so on. Every object possesses some duration of existence, has a beginning and an end, and goes through certain stages or states in its development. Some objects are only beginning to arise, others have become established and are developing, while still others are in the process of destruction.

The philosophical concept of *time* reflects the universal property of material processes to follow one after another in a definite sequence, to possess duration and develop by stages.

Space and time are *universal forms of the existence of matter.* "There is nothing in the world but matter in motion, and matter in motion cannot move otherwise than in space and time,"* Lenin wrote.

The most important attribute of space and time is their *objectivity,* i.e., independence of man's consciousness. This is natural for they are the basic forms of objectively existing matter.

Idealism denies the objectivity of space and time. Subjective idealists consider them the product of man's consciousness, while objective idealists claim that they are engendered by the absolute idea, the universal spirit.

In *Materialism and Empirio-Criticism* Lenin convincingly demonstrated the insolvency of idealist conceptions of space and time. If, he wrote, we are to believe the idealists that space and time are merely products of human reason, what happens to the incontrovertible fact, proved by science, that the Earth had existed in space and time long before the appearance of man? The Earth has been in existence for thousands of millions of

* V. I. Lenin, "Materialism and Empirio-Criticism", *Collected Works,* Vol. 14, p. 175.

years, while man only for tens of thousands of years! Clearly, this leaves no room for any "creation" of space and time by man or by some mystical absolute idea, or universal reason.

Pointing to the objectivity of space and time, dialectical materialism also reveals their other most general properties, proceeding from the premise that they are determined by the nature of matter itself. The eternity and infinity of matter thus determine the *eternity* of time and *infinity* of space. This means that they have never had a beginning and will never have an end. Modern science penetrates the distant regions of outer space and studies immense periods of time. With the aid of powerful radio telescopes astronomers study material bodies at a distance of thousands of millions of light-years from the Earth. (Light travels at a velocity of 300,000 kilometres per second.) However immense these distances, they are infinitesimally small as compared with the infinite world. Similarly minute, as compared to the eternity of the Universe, are the vast periods of time, measured in thousands of millions of years, which modern geology studies.

Space as a form of existence of matter is *tridimensional*, which means that every material body has three dimensions: length, width and height. Correspondingly, bodies can move in the three mutually perpendicular directions.

In contrast to space, time has only one dimension. That is why all bodies develop in time in one direction only, from the past to the future. Time is *irreversible*, it moves only forward and it is impossible to revert its movement, to bring back the past. This is a natural fact, yet one which is stubbornly refuted by reactionary Western politicians who endeavour to reverse the course of history and bring back the bygone era of capitalism's undivided sway in the world. But history cannot be reversed; it is impossible to turn the world of the 20th century into a world of the 19th century. Times are different now and so is the correlation of forces on the world scene. Today there is a mighty world socialist system which upholds peace, democracy, national liberation and socialism and determines the direction of social progress.

Such are the most general properties of space and time.

The Concepts of Space and Time in Natural Science

These philosophical concepts of space and time as universal forms of the existence of matter should be distinguished from the concepts about the space and time properties of concrete material objects accepted in natural science.

As science develops these concepts too are developed and specified, new properties of space and time are discovered and the dependence of these properties on the material nature of bodies is more definitely established.

Classical mechanics, recognising the objectivity of space and time, separated them from matter, and held them to be absolutely uniform and immutable. *Isaac Newton* (1643-1727), the founder of classical mechanics, for example, pictured space as a huge receptacle in which things were placed in a definite order, but these things themselves supposedly had no relation to space whatsoever.

Newton held that spatial properties of all bodies of the Universe are similar and fully covered by Euclidean geometry which is taught at school and which he regarded as the only possible, the absolute geometry.

His views of time were similarly metaphysical.

The great Russian mathematician *Nikolai Lobachevsky* (1792-1856) elaborated a new, non-Euclidean geometry, which refuted the metaphysical views of space and extended man's ideas of the spatial properties of bodies. Lobachevsky arrived at the conclusion that the properties of space are not identical in different regions of the Universe, that they depend on the nature of physical bodies and on the material processes taking place in them. Convinced that in nature there are bodies whose spatial properties do not fit into the framework of Euclidean geometry, he discovered these new properties, demonstrating specifically that on definite surfaces the sum of angles of a triangle is not equal to 180° as in Euclidean geometry, but is smaller.

The *theory of relativity,* elaborated by *Albert Einstein* (1879-1955), one of the greatest physicists of all time, is the modern theory of space and time in natural science. This theory reveals the organic connection of space and time both with each other and with matter in motion.

The *special theory of relativity* demonstrates the dependence of space and time properties of bodies on the velocity of their movement. At relatively small velocities it is impossible to trace this dependence because the space and time properties change on a scale which can be practically detected only at speeds close to that of light.

The theory of relativity shows that at speeds close to that of light the length of a moving body compared to a body in a state of rest decreases as the speed increases. Moreover, time too does not remain invariable: with the increase in speed the course of time is slowed down. These conclusions, which follow from the theory of relativity, have been corroborated experimentally. For example, the life of the meson (an elementary particle which arises during the fission of an atomic nucleus) is very short, but if its speed is increased, the "lifetime" of the meson is lengthened.

According to the theory of relativity, space and time change not by themselves but in inseparable interconnection. This connection is so firm that they form an unbreakable whole and time acquires, as it were, the role of a fourth dimension, in addition to the three dimensions of space. The theory of relativity also gives a strictly mathematical expression to the organic connection of space and time.

The *general theory of relativity* or the *theory of gravitation*, has demonstrated that the properties of space and time also depend on the presence of masses of matter. Bodies possessing a huge mass and great force of gravity produce a change in the properties of space near them; as physicists say, space "is curved". Time too changes correspondingly: it slows down.

At first glance, the conclusions of the theory of relativity seem to run counter to our customary notions about the properties of space and time. But they are true and are confirmed by scientific experiments. Their unusual character merely goes to show that in knowledge man must not confine himself to customary notions, but must go farther and deeper, and reveal the entire complexity and diversity of the material world.

We have seen that the concepts about the properties of space and time, given by natural science, undergo change. But this changeability does not in any way challenge the propositions of dialectical materialism concerning their objective existence. On the contrary, each success of science furnishes more and more proof of the objectivity of space and time, and their inseparable connection with matter in motion.

CHAPTER IV

Matter and Consciousness

In the preceding chapter we examined matter and its forms. We also learned that matter exists outside of man's consciousness and independent of it. But what is consciousness, what is its relation to matter, how does it arise? Let us examine these questions.

1. Consciousness—a Property of Highly Organised Matter

Before discussing the essence of consciousness let us recall that man's *conscious, spiritual activity* includes his thoughts and emotions, will and character, sensations, ideas, views, etc.

What is the nature and the source of all these phenomena?

Natural science and philosophy traversed a long and hard road before they were able to answer this question correctly. Contemporary science has proved that consciousness is a product of the long evolution of matter. Matter and nature have always existed, while man is a result of a relatively later development of the material world. It took millions upon millions of years before the development of matter resulted in the emergence of society and with it, man capable of thinking. Consciousness is a product of nature, a property of matter, though not of all of it, but only of *highly organised matter,* the human brain.

Consciousness, having arisen as a result of the development of matter, is inseparably bound up with it. It is indivisible from thinking matter, the brain, whose attribute it is. The celebrated Russian physiologists *Ivan Sechenov* (1829-1905) and *Ivan Pavlov* (1849-1936) established that all mental activity is based on definite material processes, namely, *physiological processes,* which transpire in the human brain, particularly in the cortex of the cerebral hemispheres. Disturbance of the normal activity of the brain, its lesion caused by disease, injury of other causes, leads to a sharp derangement in man's thinking, to a mental disorder.

Drawing on numerous experimental data, Pavlov concluded that "psychical activity is the result of the physiological activity of a certain mass of the brain".

Pavlov's doctrine of higher nervous activity confirms the fundamental thesis of dialectical materialism concerning the dependence of consciousness on matter. It convincingly demonstrates that the brain and physiological processes in it are the substratum (basis) of human consciousness and the material conditions without which thinking is impossible.

But is the human brain alone enough for the functioning of consciousness? Can it think by itself, independent of the influence of the surrounding world upon it?

No, by itself the brain is incapable of thinking. Consciousness *is inseparably bound up with man's material environment,* and it cannot function without the influence of this environment. Visual, auditory, olfactory and other sensations arise in the brain only under the influence of objectively existing objects with their intrinsic colours, smells, sounds and other properties. These objects and their properties act on the sense organs and the resultant irritation is transmitted along the nerve channels to the cortex of the cerebral hemispheres where the respective sensations arise. Sensations create perceptions, ideas and also concepts and other forms of thought. All of them represent only *images,* more or less exact reflections of objectively existing objects and phenomena. Outside of them these images cannot arise in man's consciousness. This means that ability to *reflect* the material world is the specific distinction of consciousness as a property of the brain.

Needless to say, not only images of existing objects and phenomena arise in man's consciousness, but also images of things which are not yet in existence. For instance, man creates images of future buildings, machines and many other artificial things, and also images of future social order, etc. But these images arise on the basis of reflection of what *already exists, in* the basis of the knowledge of the surrounding objective reality, its potentialities and trends of development.

Thus, in answer to the question about the nature of consciousness we can say that *man's consciousness is a special property of highly organised matter, the brain, to reflect material reality.*

Insolvency of Vulgar Materialism and Idealism

Since consciousness is inseparable from highly organised matter and is its product, then is it not a variety of matter and identical to it? That, precisely, is what vulgar materialists maintain.* Speculating in the indivisibility of consciousness and matter, they also consider them identical and assert, in particular, that the relation of thought to the brain is approxi-

---

* Vulgar materialism is a philosophical trend which originated in Germany in the mid-19th century.

mately the same as that of gall to the liver, and that the brain allegedly secretes thought.

Being fully consistent with the achievements of natural sciences,dialectical materialism rejects the vulgar-materialist understanding of consciousness. Although consciousness is connected with definite material physiological processes, it cannot be reduced to these·processes. Thought is inseparable from matter, from the brain, but it must not be identified with matter. Lenin held that to regard thought as material means to make a wrong step towards confusing materialism with idealism.

Thought is not a thing, it cannot be seen or photographed. Thought is the *image* of objects and phenomena existing in the world. It is an ideal and not a material image. It is not a simple photograph of reality, not a lifeless copy of it. Marx wrote about thought that "the ideal is nothing else than the material world reflected by the human mind, and translated into forms of thought".** Reality, acting in man, always passes through the prism of the laws governing thought, such as *analysis* and *synthesis, generalisations* etc... What sets man apart from animals is his ability to think, i.e., to actively reflect reality, to influence it, to set himself certain aims and work for their achievement.

Dialectical materialism rejects the vulgar-materialist understanding of consciousness. It regards as a profound mistake the assertion that consciousness or thought is an attribute of all matter. The great Dutch philosopher Spinoza, for example, held that consciousness is as much a necessary attribute (property) of all nature as extension, corporeality.

This view is wrong, because it ignores the qualitative differences between inorganic and organic matter (thinking matter in particular). Lenin held that sensation in a clearly manifest form is inherent only in higher, organic forms of matter, whereas all matter possesses only the property of *reflection,* i.e., the ability to react in a definite way to external influences. To a certain extent this property is akin to sensation, but is not identical with it and therefore consciousness cannot be regarded as a property of all matter.

Speculating on the ideal nature of consciousness, idealists maintain that it exists on its own, independent of matter. Their line of reasoning runs as follows: if thought is ideal, is not a thing and therefore cannot be found in the human brain, it is consequently not connected with matter or the brain, and exists independently. It is allegedly not only independent of matter, but

* Karl Marx, *Capital,* Vol. 1, Moscow, 1974, p. 29.

even "creates" it. Idealists refuse to see behind thought its prototype, the things and objects of the objective world.

Attempts to divorce thought from the brain are also absolutely untenable. Lenin aptly called a philosophy which endeavours to do so and asserts that thought exists without the brain a "brainless" philosophy. Natural science, Lenin wrote, firmly upholds that consciousness does not exist independently of the body, that it is secondary, a function of the brain, a reflection of the outside world.

At the same time Lenin maintained that there was no absolute antithesis between consciousness and matter, that it is absolute only within the framework of the fundamental question of philosophy, i.e., of the question what is primary, matter or consciousness. Outside the limits of the fundamental question of philosophy this antithesis is relative. In the first place this is manifested in the fact that consciousness is a property of highly organised matter, arises and develops under the influence of material factors, and, in the second place, in the fact that, having arisen on the basis of matter, consciousness acquires a degree of independence and actively influences the development of the material world.

Consciousness and Cybernetics

The world is witnessing the rapid development of a new science, *cybernetics* which studies various control systems and control process, and has created some remarkable machines. Some of them guide trains, aircraft or intricate production processes, others translate texts from one language into another, still others perform logical operations, extremely complex mathematical calculations, etc. These machines can be fed information, "memorise" and process it and perform useful functions. In some respects these machines surpass man: for instance, they perform calculations hundreds of thousands of times faster than man, study a vast amount of data, analyse a mass of variants, and so forth. Machines are being designed which will be able to perfect the programme of their work and even improve its own structure on the basis of preceding activity. A machine can operate where man cannot work either due to danger (for instance in places where atomic and other harmful processes take place), or inaccessibility (remote outer space).

The progress of cybernetics has given grounds to ascribe to automatic machines the ability to experience sensations and even to think. Moreover, there is talk that it is possible to develop an automatic machine whose intellectual capacity will enable it to surpass, and, in the final count, to replace man. It is claimed that the era of robots will replace the era of mankind.

In reality, even the most perfect machine cannot experience sensations, let alone think. A machine does not think, it merely *imitates* or *models* certain logical functions inherent in man, and only those of them which can be formalised or mathematically processed. The fact that as science progresses the range of thinking operations which can be formalised broadens does not change the essence of matter: man and man alone is capable of thought, which is a property of the brain as a specially organised matter, a product of the prolonged evolution of the material world and, above all, of the social environment. Thought is social in nature, while a machine, no matter how perfect, has been and will always be a lifeless mechanism created and controlled by man.

Man singles himself out from nature, he actively cognises the surrounding world, and influences and transforms it. He possesses inexhaustible creative powers and an amazingly profound and broad range of sensations, thoughts, emotions, interests, etc. The machine is deprived of all this. It is the product of the astute mind and skilled hands of man who programmes its functions no matter how difficult or amazing they may be.

Just as an ordinary machine facilitates man's physical efforts, the cybernetic machine facilitates his mental efforts, freeing his mind from the need to perform tiring, monotonous and uncreative operations, and broadens his intellectual abilities. But however high the level which cybernetics may attain in its development, an automatic machine will never become a vehicle of human consciousness and will never replace man as a social being. It will always remain an instrument, a means of solving production and cognitive problems confronting mankind.

Now let us examine the origin and development of consciousness.

2. Consciousness—a Product of the Development of Matter. The Origin and Development of Consciousness

As we pointed out earlier, all matter possesses the intrinsic general property of *reflection*, i.e., the *ability to reconstruct itself internally under external influences, to react to them accordingly*. Reflection is always connected with the interaction of two (or more) bodies: the acting one and the one subjected to the action. That is why the *character* of reflection depends both on external influences and on the internal state of the body reacting to the influence.

If we examine an inorganic body, a living organism and man from this point of view we find that they reflect the world differently.

Simple, *passive* reflection is inherent in an inorganic body. Such a body does not differentiate between the factors of the environment, does not single out the favourable ones and is incapable of protecting itself from the unfavourable ones.

A living organism reacts differently to external influences. It *adapts* itself to the environment, reacts in a different way to various external stimuli, making use of favourable factors and avoiding unnecessary, harmful ones. Here we have *active, selective,* but so far unconscious reflection.

We find a qualitatively new, higher form of reflection in man who possesses the ability to *consciously* reflect reality. He not only adapts himself to the environment, but acts upon it, transforms it on the basis of the knowledge he has gained.

To establish the *origin of consciousness* amounts to tracing how, during the transition from inorganic matter to living matter and thence to thinking matter (the human brain), the non-living, passive reflection turned into active, selective reflection inherent in everything living, and how the ability to think developed from the latter.

From Inorganic to Living Matters and Thence to Thinking Matter

Natural sciences command a vast array of facts showing that *living nature arose out of non-living,* inorganic nature. There is no impassable boundary between them. Chemical analysis shows that both inorganic bodies and living organisms are formed from the same chemical elements. Organisms contain large quantities of hydrogen, oxygen, nitrogen and particularly carbon, which comprises the basis of the chemical composition of living organisms and the products of their vital processes.

Scientists have put forward the hypothesis that the primary gas-dust matter from which our Earth was formed originally contained the simplest compounds of carbon and hydrogen, *hydrocarbons,* from which the more complex organic compounds were subsequently formed. Entering into chemical associations with each other, the organic compounds became more and more complex until *amino acids,* the basic elements of the *protein* molecules, were formed. As organic substances became more differentiated and complex, their reflective ability became more diverse and intricate.

Hundreds of millions of years later the molecules of this primary chemical protein, formed from amino acids, had turned into a living protein body and thereby acquired the property of metabolism, which is the basic feature of everything living. Landing in a favourable environment and entering into a metabolic interchange with it, this protein body became an *organism*.

Metabolism is a contradictory process of *assimilation* (absorption of nutritive substances from the environment and their conversion into the living cells and tissues of an organism) and *dissimilation* (disintegration, destruction of this living tissue). This process is inherent only in living protein, in an organism. Metabolic exchange with the environment and constant self-regeneration differentiate the simplest living organism from the most complex non-living body. Only by assimilating nutritive substances and excreting the products of their disintegration, can an organism live and develop. "Life is the mode of existence of protein bodies, the essential element of which consists in *continual metabolic exchange with the natural environment outside them,* and which ceases with the cessation of this metabolism,"* Engels points out.

The coming into being of the first simplest organisms was a tremendous step forward in the development of reflection, a general intrinsic property of matter, in the emergence of consciousness. Reflection of reality, inherent in inorganic nature, turned into a qualitatively new, *biological* reflection. The simplest form of biological reflection is *response to stimuli, irritability,* which is inherent in all organisms and serves as a means of their orientation, or adaptability to the external environment.

Plants, for example, are especially sensitive to sunlight. They literally reach out for it; for them light is the source of life. The simplest monocellular organism, the amoeba, reacts to food stimuli, but if it has just swallowed food, the food stimuli have no effect upon it. This means that the amoeba, like any other organism possessing the property of responding to stimuli, reflects the outside world not passively, but *selectively.* Its organism, as it were, gravitates towards useful, needed stimuli and shuns harmful, unnecessary ones.

But its selective power is not great. A simple organism has neither organs nor tissues, nor cells, specially receptive to particular forms of stimuli. It responds to outside excitations in its entirety.

In the course of further evolution, as the organisms themselves and the environment became more complex, an even higher form of reflection, *sensation,* arose on the basis of response to stimuli. Like response to stimuli, sensation was a result of the action of the outside world on the organism, but here the range of external stimuli to which the organism

* Frederick Engels, *Dialectics of Nature*, p. 301.

responded in one way or another broadened considerably. The organism reacted to colour, smell and sound, it developed the sensations of taste, cold, heat, moisture and responded to mechanical, physical and other influences. Organs capable of perceiving only a definite range of external influences (colour, sound, smell, etc.) appeared in the organism. Subsequently, as the organisms developed, their sensations became more subtle and diverse. The adaptability of the organism to the environment increased and a special organ for maintaining contact with the environment, the central nervous system, came into being.

In the field of biology the study of *reflexes* has graphically shown that lower and higher animals do not have the same ability to reflect the surrounding world, to adapt to the environment. Reflexes are responsive reactions of the organism to external influences, as well as to its own internal changes. All of them are divided into unconditioned and conditioned reflexes. *Unconditioned reflexes* are inherent in all organisms, both lower and higher, and are inborn, hereditary. A man instantly draws away his hand if it is touched by something hot—this is an unconditioned reflex. The intricate intertwining of unconditioned reflexes forms instincts (sex, food and others), which play a major role in the life and development of an organism.

Higher animals, however, also have *conditioned reflexes* which are of a temporary nature and are formed in definite conditions. If for a certain time a dog is fed to the accompaniment of the ringing of a bell, there will come a moment when the dog reacts to the ringing of a bell in the same way as when it is fed: saliva will be secreted. A temporary connection has been formed in the brain of the dog whereby the sound of the bell has become the signal for food. All other conditioned reflexes are formed on the same principle. Thanks to them the organism adapts itself very delicately to the environment and is very sensitive to its influences. The conditioned reflexes which acquire particular importance for the organism become fixed and turn into unconditioned ones; on the basis of the latter new temporary connections arise, part of which again become fixed. Hence, in the course of the evolution of living organisms, psyche progressed continuously, and this ultimately led to sentient matter acquiring the ability to *think*.

Decisive Role of Labour in the Rise of Consciousness

Both man and higher animals possess the intrinsic ability to experience sensations. This ability, according to Pavlov, rests on a physiological basis which is common for both man and animals, namely, the *first signal system*. It is a mechanism through which the organism responds directly to the action of concrete objects and phenomena. Being the sole signals for an animal, these objects act on its sense organs and arouse corresponding sensations in its nervous system.

But man's sensations, in contrast to those of animals, are always illuminated by the light of reason. Man is capable of *abstract thinking*, i.e., of a generalised reflection of reality in concepts expressed in *words*. Every word denotes a definite object, phenomenon, or action with which it is inseparably associated. That is why man reacts to words just as to the direct influence of the objects themselves. Inasmuch as the first signals are the objects themselves, the words designating them acquire the role of secondary signals. They, as Pavlov pointed out, are the "signals of signals". He called the physiological mechanism through which man reacts to words, to speech, the *second signal system* This system is inherent in man alone.

The first and the second signal systems are organically connected, giving man an all-round and profound knowledge of reality.

And so, man's consciousness qualitatively differs from the mentality of animals.

The cause of this difference lies in the fact that the mentality of animals is a product of biological development only, whereas man's consciousness is above all a result of *historical, social* development.

The very sensations of man radically differ from those of animals. The eyes of an eagle, for example, see much farther than those of man, but man has immeasurably greater insight than the eagle into what is seen.

Marx held that the formation of man's five sense organs is a product of the whole of world history. Man's musical ear, his eye for nature's beauty, his fine taste and other sense organs have developed on the basis of the practical experience of human society at various stages of its history.

Labour, i.e., production of material values, is the decisive factor in the development of man, in the emergence and development of his consciousness. "Labour created man himself," Engels pointed out. Due to labour our distant ape-like ancestor developed into the modern man, *Homo Sapiens*. Labour gave man food, clothing, shelter and not only protected him against the elements, but also enabled him to subjugate them, to place them at his service. Through labour man changed himself beyond recognition and also changed our planet. Labour is man's greatest possession and is indispensable to his life and development.

Anthropoid apes already had the prerequisites of labour. They used sticks, stones and other objects to procure food. But they did it unconsciously and accidentally. Neither apes nor any other animals can make even the simplest tool. Man, however, consciously makes and uses tools, and in this lays the qualitative distinction of his labour. To learn this man needed hundreds of thousands of years, throughout which there took place the highly intricate process of man's emergence and the formation and development of his consciousness.

The adoption of a vertical posture by anthropoid apes was of great importance in creating conditions for labour and the appearance of the first glimmers of consciousness. This posture meant that the front limbs were relieved of their use as an aid to walking and could now be used for work. At first, with the help of his hands, our distant ancestor used "implements" of labour (sticks and stones) in their natural state and then began to make tools out of natural objects. The first of them were extremely primitive (a roughly-hewn stone, a sharpened stick, etc.). The consciousness of the man of that age was primitive too. He did not yet distinguish the essence of objects, did not see what they had in common, did not know how they could be of use to him.

The further development and improvement of labour was accompanied by an advance in man's consciousness. Coming in contact with various natural objects in the course of obtaining his means of subsistence, he learned their properties, compared them and singled out what they had in common and what recurred.

The making and improvement of labour implements played a particularly important role in the development of consciousness. The implements, which were handed down from generation to generation, embodied work habits and knowledge. Succeeding generations, knowing the methods of making and using the implements of their ancestors, were able to improve and develop them.

The consciousness of primitive man was organically bound up with his labour; it was, so to say, interwoven with his labour activity. And this is understandable because man first of all learned that which was directly connected with his labour, the satisfaction of his wants. It is no accident that the portrayal of man's labour occurs so often in primitive art.

In the process of labour man acquired not only consciousness, i.e., ability to reflect the surrounding world, but also *self-consciousness,* i.e., awareness and the ability to assess his thoughts and sentiments, interests, motives and deeds, and his place and role in society. This, in turn, prompted the further improvement of his work habits and the establishment and development of society.

Thus, in unity of labour and thought, and on the basis of labour activity, man's consciousness developed and improved.

Language and Thought

Language, articulate speech, was of great importance in forming man's consciousness. Language, which arose together with consciousness on the basis of labour, played a very great part in enabling man to emerge from the animal kingdom, to develop his thinking and organise material production. Labour has always been social. From the first days of their existence people had to unite to fight the mighty forces of nature, to wrest the means of livelihood from it. That is why in the process of labour there arose the need for *communication* between people, the need to *tell* each other something. Through this pressing need the undeveloped larynx of the ape was transformed into an organ capable of uttering articulate sounds. That was how articulate speech or language came into existence.

Marx called language the *direct reality of thought*. And did so because thought can exist only in the material shell of the word, or a substitute sign, or symbol. Whether a man thinks to himself, voices his thoughts aloud, or puts them down in writing, the thought is always vested in words. Thanks to language, thoughts are not only formed, but also transmitted and perceived. In words and combinations of words man fixes the results of reflection of the objective world in his consciousness, which not only enables people to exchange thoughts, but also to pass them on from one generation to another. Without speech and written language, the priceless experience of many generations would be lost and each new generation would be compelled to begin anew the very hard process of studying the world.

Language is not connected with reality directly, but through thought. Hence, at times it is not easy to establish the direct connection of a given word with a specific material object. In different languages and even in one language frequently the same word denotes various objects, or various words denote the same object. All this creates the illusion that language is independent of reality.

This illusion is pursued by the *semantic idealists*, proponents of a trend in contemporary bourgeois philosophy. They sever language from thought and thought from reality, maintaining that words are coined by man arbitrarily and do not designate anything real, that words are mere combinations of sounds. From this premise some seek to prove that contemporary capitalism, exploitation, aggression, etc., are merely empty words or sounds. People, they claim, only have to replace these words by others for all sources of social conflict to vanish, for all vices of contemporary capitalism to disappear.

Words are not coined by people arbitrarily, however; they are attached to definite objects and phenomena in the process of knowledge and practical activity. These objective processes are neither altered nor eliminated by the replacement of words. The apologists of capitalism, for example, have coined dozens of sweet-sounding words for describing contemporary capitalist society: "people's capitalism", "affluent society", "industrial society", etc. But these words have not abolished capitalism and its exploitation, unemployment and class antagonisms, national oppression and wars. Capitalism will disappear only as a result of the proletariat's struggle against the bourgeoisie, as a result of socialist revolution.

Consciousness is, thus, a product of the evolution of matter. But having arisen on the basis of matter, it actively influences the latter's development.

In an effort to discredit materialism, idealists claim that since materialists take matter as the basis of everything existing and maintain that things exist objectively, independent of consciousness, they underestimate the role of consciousness, and regard it only as a passive reflection of being.

Dialectical materialism, however, does not in the least underestimate the role of consciousness in the development of matter, of being. As a product of matter and as its reflection, consciousness does not remain passive, but *actively influences* the world. It is in this sense that Lenin wrote that "man's consciousness not only reflects the objective world, but creates it".*

This does not mean, of course, that consciousness directly influences being, or that it creates the world; by itself, thought is incapable of moving even the tiniest blade of grass. What is meant is that consciousness, if it reflects the world correctly, can serve as a *guide* in man's creative work in transforming life.

The active role of consciousness, particularly in the life of society, will be examined in greater detail in later chapters.

---

* V. I. Lenin, "Philosophical Notebooks", *Collected Works*, Vol. 38, p. 212.

CHAPTER V

Marxist Dialectics as the Theory of Development and Universal Connection

The philosophy of Marxism is dialectical materialism, in which materialism and dialectics are indissolubly interconnected. In the preceding chapters we have examined the essence of Marxist philosophical materialism. Our task now is to analyse in detail *Marxist materialist dialectics* and its practical significance.

1. Dialectics—Theory of Development

Marxist dialectics, as we have pointed out, examines the world in constant movement, change and development. Our daily experience, the development of science and the history of society convince us that all objects and phenomena of the world are not immutable.

Everything in the world *develops*. The innumerable bodies of the Universe, the solar system, the Earth and everything on it are the product of the long development of matter. Man himself also arose in the process of evolution of the material world.

Human society too is developing. This is vividly demonstrated by the present century, the age of great historical progress and unprecedented social change. The capitalist system is crumbling and a new, socialist society is inexorably coming to take its place. The socialist system has already struck root in a considerable part of the world. This system is steadily developing and accumulating strength, displaying its advantages and vast potentialities. Imperialism's colonial system has disintegrated, and in fierce struggle against colonialism, scores of nations have gained independence.

We are witnessing a tremendous revolution in science and technology. Man has penetrated the depths of the atom and harnessed its mighty energy. The bounds of outer space are receding in the face of omnipotent human reason.

In reflecting the development of the material world, the consciousness of people, their ideas, theories and views change as well.

Thus, constant development, the passage of objects and phenomena from one state into another, their supersession, represent an important feature of the material world. Hence, to gain knowledge of objects and phenomena, it is necessary first of all to study their constant change and development. To really know an object we must examine it in its development, "self-movement", change.

Study of the general picture of the world's development is an important task of materialist dialectics. Dialectics, Engels wrote, is "the science of the general laws of motion and development of nature, human society and thought".*

How does Marxist dialectics understand the process of development as such?

It regards development as movement from the lower to the higher, from the simple to the complex, as a leap-like, revolutionary process. Moreover, this movement proceeds not along a closed circuit, but in the form of a spiral, each spire being deeper, richer and more diverse than the preceding one. Dialectics sees the sources of development in the intrinsic contradictions of objects and phenomena. Only Marxist dialectics furnishes the correct, truly scientific understanding of the process of development.

The basic laws of materialist dialectics give a general picture of the development of the world, its cognition and transformation. The *law of the unity and conflict of opposites* reveals the sources, the driving forces of development. The *law of the passage of quantitative into qualitative changes* indicates the leap-like, revolutionary change of the world, the continuous transformation of intrinsic quantitative changes of objects into fundamental qualitative changes. The *law of negation of the negation* characterises the progressive, spiral-like character of development. All these laws will be examined in the next chapter.

Invincibility of the New

The development of the material world is an interminable process of the dying off of the old and the emergence of the *new.* The history of the Earth's crust, for example, is the history of the formation of ever new geological structures. In the vegetable and animal kingdoms old organic forms give way to new and better ones. Just as cells are constantly regenerated in living organisms (old ones die and new ones arise) so in society too the obsolete forms of social structure die and new, progressive ones are born.

---

* Frederick Engels, *Anti-Dühring,* p. 172.

The advanced, the new is thus constantly coming to the fore to succeed the old, and nothing can prevent this process. The *invincibility of the new* is the prime feature in the development of nature, society and thought.

Marxist dialectics, however, does not regard every new phenomenon or everything that claims to be new, as truly new. Imperialist and reactionary forces, for instance, portray their economic expansion in the developing countries as a "new" policy, as assistance to their peoples. In reality this "assistance" is merely a new form of colonialism, or neocolonialism.

The new is that which is progressive, improved and viable, which constantly grows and develops. At first the new is usually quite weak and at times hardly noticeable, while the old prevails and seems invincible. Nevertheless, the old deteriorates and dies, while the new develops and triumphs in bitter struggle against the old.

After the Second World War the first small groups of the progressive-minded military appeared in the Ethiopian army. They were no match for the monarchy and the overwhelming majority of the military who supported it. Gradually, however, these groups gained in strength and number. On September 12, 1974, with the backing of the working masses, they deposed the Ethiopian monarch.

Why is the new invincible?

The new is invincible above all because it *stems from the very course of development of reality* and best of all corresponds to the objective conditions. Long ago, for example, plants with seeds that had no protective shell (so-called gymnospermous plants) predominated on Earth. Then new plants appeared, better adapted to the environment. Their seeds were reliably protected from the vagaries of the weather and this made them greatly superior to the other species. As a result these plants ousted the older species, rapidly spread over the Earth and changed the entire appearance of its vegetation.

The invincibility of the new is particularly apparent in social development. The new in society triumphs because it *corresponds to the requirements of economic life,* of material production. The socialist system is gaining the upper hand over capitalism because it provides scope for the development of the productive forces and eliminates private capitalist property, the big barrier in their way.

The new *meets the interest of the advanced, progressive classes* of society and that is why they fight vigorously for its victory. Currently national democratic revolutions which are a new, progressive stage in social development, are under way in some Asian, African and Latin American countries. A revolution is in the interests of the working class, of all working people; they naturally support it and become more and more involved in it, and that is an earnest of its victory.

The new in social development is also invincible because its *social basis is constantly growing, expanding*. The new, as it emerges, rallies round itself the most progressive forces of society. The world socialist system, which enjoys the support and respect of all progressive-minded people of the world, is a mighty centre of attraction for contemporary progressive forces. Its alliance with the international working-class and national liberation movement is an important factor of the invincibility of the world revolutionary process.

The invincibility of the new does not mean that its victory comes of itself, automatically. This victory must be prepared, must be doggedly fought for. The *conscious activity* of the people, the advanced classes, the progressive parties plays a decisive part in the victory of the new over the old in social life.

2. Dialectics—Theory of Universal Connection

The material world is not only a developing, but also a *connected, integral whole*. All its objects and phenomena develop not of themselves, not in isolation, but in inseverable connection or unity with other objects and phenomena. Each of them acts on other objects and phenomena and itself is subjected to reciprocal influence.

Science provides extensive data proving the interconnection and interdependence of phenomena and objects. Some elementary particles, for example, interacting with each other, form atoms. But atoms too are not isolated; entering into connections, they form molecules and the latter, in turn, form macroscopic bodies. The interaction of macrobodies is proved by the law of gravitation. According to this law, the Earth is connected with the Sun and other planets of the solar system and the latter is connected with still larger cosmic formations.

Living organisms are bound by an intricate chain of interaction: separate plants and also animals form species, species are united in genera, classes, etc. Organisms are connected not only among themselves, but also with the environment from which they get their necessary nutrition and energy.

The Russian scientist *Kliment Timiryazev* (1843-1920) discovered the connection of plants with the life-giving energy of the Sun. He showed that under the influence of solar energy carbon dioxide is decomposed in the chlorophyll of the green leaves of plants. The carbon is assimilated by the plant, while the oxygen, indispensable to man's respiration, is released into the air. The resultant organic substances accumulate solar energy in the form of chemical energy, which is then utilised by man when he uses plants either as food or fuel. "The green leaf, or more exactly, the microscopic green granule of chlorophyll," Timiryazev wrote "is the focus, the point in world space to which solar energy flows at one end, while all manifestations of life on Earth take their source at the other end. The plant is the connecting link between heaven and Earth. It is truly the Prometheus who stole fire from heaven. The stolen sun ray shines both in the tiny flame of a burning splinter and in the dazzling spark of electricity. The sun ray is the source of energy for the monstrous fly-wheel of a gigantic steam engine, of the artist's brush and the poet's pen."

Man is connected with nature through material production. This connection is effected through labour, an indispensable condition of man's existence. Thanks to labour man wins from nature his means of subsistence. In the process of labour the economic, production relations of people take shape and give rise to other connections, including political, legal and moral.

Thus, *universal connection and interdependence* of objects and phenomena are an essential distinctive feature of the material world. Therefore, as Lenin pointed out, in order to gain real knowledge of an object it is necessary to study all its aspects and connections. *The study of the world as an integral connected whole, examination of the universal connections of things* is an important task of materialist dialectics.

Since objects and phenomena of the material world are diverse, their interconnection, interaction are also diverse. Marxist dialectics studies not all, but only *the most general* connections, i.e., those which exist in all spheres of the material and spiritual world.

The laws and categories of materialist dialectics are a reflection of these connections in man's consciousness.

Knowledge of connections is of tremendous importance because, by revealing them, people discover the *laws* of the objective world. Knowledge of these laws is an indispensable requisite for the practical activity of people. It is the task of science to disclose these laws and place them at the disposal of man. Let us give a more detailed explanation of law.

Concept of Law

Very many laws operate in the objective world. There are laws of inorganic nature and the organic world, of society and thought. But laws in any sphere of reality have certain features in common which are covered by the *philosophical concept of law*. What are these features?

To begin with, a law is a *relation* or *connection* between developing objects or aspects of these objects. A law, however, is not any connection, but only a *stable, recurrent connection*, inherent not in one object or a small group of objects, but in a vast mass of objects and phenomena. For example, the periodic law, discovered by *Dmitri Mendeleyev* (1834-1907), indicates the dependence of the properties of all chemical elements on the magnitude of the positive charge of the nucleus. A law, thus, is not a single, but a *general* connection between phenomena.

Another important feature of a law is that it does not represent all recurrent connections, but only those which are *necessary* and *essential*. The biological law of the interconnection of an organism and the environment fixes the necessary, important connection of the organism with the conditions of its existence.

Being necessary, essential in phenomena, a law operates only if there are the appropriate conditions which bring about not any, but a basically *definite* course of events. Strict definiteness in the operation of laws is of great practical importance: a knowledge of the laws and direction of development helps people to foresee the future. For instance, an understanding of the laws of social development and the conditions in which they operate enables people to control social processes and foresee the course of historical events.

Thus, a *law is an essential and necessary, general and recurrent connection among phenomena of the material world*, which brings about a definite course of events.

A struggle over the question of the character of laws has been in progress between materialism and idealism for a long time now. Idealists hold that laws are made either by man or by a mythical "absolute idea", "a universal spirit". In the final analysis, this standpoint leads to recognition of the divine origin of laws and to the assertion that every law of nature is a law of God, every power in nature is a deed of God.

In contrast to idealism, dialectical materialism proceeds from recognition of the *objective character* of laws. This means that man is unable to make or change laws at will, he can only cognise, reflect them. The world is matter moving in conformity to law, Lenin wrote, and our consciousness, being the highest product of nature, is in a position only to *reflect* this conformity to law.

The objectivity of laws also implies that they operate independently of the will and desires of man and therefore any attempt to act contrary to laws is foredoomed. For example, it is impossible to ignore the law of gravitation and to go into outer space without overcoming the Earth's gravity. Nor is it possible to ignore the laws of social development. This, for example, is attested to by the futility of the desperate attempts made by the imperialists to halt the inexorable process of the mankind's development from capitalism to socialism.

Dialectical materialism, attacking the idealist conception of laws, also rejects *fatalism* (from Latin *fatalis,* meaning decreed by destiny), i.e., blind worship of laws, disbelief in the power of human reason and the ability of people to cognise laws and make use of them. Man cannot abolish or create laws, but he is able to cognise them and utilise them in his practical activity. Knowledge of nature's laws enables man not only to control the destructive action of water, wind and other natural elements, but also to make them serve his needs. Drawing on the laws of social development, people transform social life.

The most favourable conditions for learning and applying laws are provided by the socialist system where the operation of the laws governing social development coincides with the interests of all the people, where the dominance of socialist property enables society to use the natural resources in a planned way and purposefully to improve social relations. Let us take, for example, the law of planned, proportionate development of the economy under socialism. Knowledge and application of this law are necessary, inasmuch as socialist production cannot be developed without a plan. At the same time this law fully corresponds to the interests of the working people, because socialist production is developed for the purpose of satisfying ever more fully their constantly growing material and cultural requirements. That is why the working people are interested in cognising this law and placing it at their service. One of the main tasks facing the national democratic revolutions in socialist-oriented countries is that of organising centralised national planning based on socialist principles.

3. Significance of Marxist Dialectics

Marxist materialist dialectics is a profound and all-embracing theory of development and universal connection. By giving a general idea of material processes it comprises a *scientific method of cognising the world* and helps man to comprehend the most diverse phenomena of reality. But in addition to being a method of knowledge, Marxist dialectics is also an instrument of the *revolutionary transformation of the world,* and is of enormous importance for the practical activity of the working class and its Marxist party.

Materialist dialectics is basically *critical* and *revolutionary.* It maintains that nothing is immutable or eternal. Nothing, with the exception of infinite progress, perpetual and inexorable advance, can stand up to it.

It is an irreconcilable opponent of metaphysics and reaction, of all attempts to defend the moribund social system and perpetuate private property and exploitation, wars and national oppression. It helped to discover the historically transitory nature of capitalism and proved the inevitability of its doom and replacement by the new, socialist system. That is why it is regarded with hatred and horror by the bourgeoisie and its ideologists.

Being critical and revolutionary, Marxist dialectics is wholly consistent with the revolutionary spirit of the working class and its Marxist party, with the turbulent, dynamic nature of the contemporary epoch. It substantiates and illumines the steadfast struggle of the working class and its Marxist party against imperialism, for peace, democracy, national liberation and socialism.

Marxist dialectics rejects everything backward and obsolete; it does not tolerate stereotyped practices, stagnation and dogmatism in theoretical thought. It demands farsightedness and reliance on progressive social forces. That is what the CPSU does.

CHAPTER VI

Basic Laws of Materialist Dialectics

Marxist dialectics is the teaching of development and universal connection. The main thing in development is the question of its *sources*, its *driving forces*. Since the answer to this question is furnished by the law of the unity and conflict of opposites, we shall begin with this law in our exposition of the basic laws of materialist dialectics.

The Law of the Unity and Conflict of Opposites

Lenin called the law of the unity and conflict of opposites the *essence*, the *core* of dialectics. This law reveals the sources, the real causes of the eternal motion and development of the material world. Knowledge of this law is of fundamental importance for understanding the dialectics of development of nature, society and thought, for science and revolutionary practice.

An analysis of the contradictions in objective reality and disclosure of their nature are a major requisite for Marxist scientific study and practical action.

1. The Unity and Conflict of Opposites

Before discussing the law of the unity and conflict of opposites as such, let us see how Marxist-Leninist dialectics understands "opposites", the "unity" of opposites.

The Unity of Opposites

All of us have used an ordinary magnet at one time or another and we know that its main feature is that it has a *north* and *a south* poles which are mutually exclusive and at the same time interconnected. However hard we try to separate the north pole of a magnet from the south pole, we shall not succeed. Even if it is divided into two, four, eight or more parts a magnet will still possess the same two poles.

Opposites are, then, the internal sides, tendencies, forces of an object, which are mutually exclusive but at the same time presuppose each other.

The inseverable interconnection of these sides makes up the *unity of opposites.*

All objects and phenomena have contradictory sides which are organically connected, make up the indissoluble unity of opposites. In the centre of the atom there is the positively charged nucleus surrounded by negatively charged electrons. The chemical process is a contradictory unity of association and dissociation of atoms.

There are opposites in living organisms as well. Recall the opposite processes of assimilation and dissimilation which constitute the process of metabolism inherent in living matter. In addition, organisms also have such intrinsic contradictory properties as heredity and adaptability. Heredity is the tendency of the organism to preserve hereditarily acquired characteristics; adaptability, on the other hand, is the ability to develop new characteristics corresponding to the changed conditions.

Man's mental activity is marked by the opposite processes of excitation and inhibition, concentration and irradiation of excitation in the cortex of the cerebral hemispheres.

Societies dominated by private property relations have opposite classes—the slaves and slave-owners in slave society; the serfs and feudal lords under feudalism, the proletariat and bourgeoisie under capitalism.

Contradictory sides are also inherent in the process of knowledge. Man employs such opposite and interconnected methods of study as induction and deduction, analysis and synthesis, etc.

Contradictoriness of objects and phenomena of the world is thus of a *general, universal* nature. There is no object or phenomenon in the world which could not be divided into opposites.

Opposites are not only mutually exclusive, but also necessarily *presuppose* each other. They coexist in one object or phenomenon and are inconceivable one without the other. We have already mentioned the inseverable unity of the opposite poles of a magnet. Similarly inseparable are assimilation and dissimilation in living organisms, and analysis and synthesis in the process of knowledge. Capitalist society is impossible without opposite classes—the proletariat and bourgeoisie. As long as capitalism lasts, the worker is forced to hire himself out to the capitalist, and the capitalist always tries to exploit the worker to the maximum.

"And it is just as impossible to have one side of contradiction without the other," Engels wrote, "as it is to retain the whole of an apple in one's hand after half has been eaten."*

The Conflict of Opposites Is the Source of Development

And so, objects and phenomena are a unity of opposites. What is the *character* of this unity? Do opposites peacefully coexist in this unity or do they enter into contradiction, into struggle with each other?

The development of the most diverse objects and phenomena shows that opposite sides cannot coexist peacefully in one object: the contradictory, mutually exclusive character of opposites necessarily causes a *struggle* between them. The old and the new, the emergent and the obsolete must come into contradiction, must clash. *It is contradiction, the conflict of opposites that is the main source of development of matter and consciousness.* "Development is the 'struggle' of opposites," wrote Lenin.** He stressed that this conflict is absolute, just as development or motion is absolute.

The proposition that the conflict of opposites is decisive in development in no way belittles the importance of their unity. The unity of opposites is a *necessary condition* of the conflict, because it takes place only where opposite sides exist in one object or phenomenon.

Lenin pointed out that a state of temporary equilibrium could also exist between opposites; this means that, at a certain stage in the development of a process, neither side predominates.

In any process the equilibrium of opposites is relative because, if it were constant, eternal, there would be no development in the world at all. Conflict alone is the source, the driving force of development.

Many modern bourgeois philosophers distort the revolutionary essence of the core of Marxist dialectics by regarding the equilibrium of opposites as absolute and by denying the conflict of opposites. They see the main thing not in the conflict of opposites, but in their reconciliation, their equilibrium. Thereby, bourgeois ideologists, in fulfilment of the instructions of the capitalists, endeavour to perpetuate capitalist society, reconcile the interests of the bourgeoisie and the proletariat and in this way divert the people from the struggle for socialism, from striving to resolve the profound contradictions of capitalism by revolution.

---

* Frederick Engels, "The Origin of the Family, Private Property and the State", International Publishers, New York, 1970, p. 130.
** V.I. Lenin, "On the Question of Dialectics", *Collected Works*, Vol. 38, p. 358.

In reality, however, it is impossible to reconcile class contradictions; this is convincingly shown by the entire history of mankind, and by the revolutionary struggle of the working class.

The history of science and of society proves that the conflict of opposites is the source of development. Yet we must bear in mind that in different spheres of the material world this conflict is manifested in different ways.

The conflict (interaction) of such opposite forces as attraction and repulsion is prevalent in inorganic nature. The interaction of mechanical, electrical and nuclear forces of attraction and repulsion plays a very great part in the rise and existence of atomic nuclei, atoms and molecules. The conflict of these forces, as modern cosmogonic theories show, was the most important source in the birth of the solar system.

Modern astronomy has also demonstrated that the interaction of forces of attraction and repulsion is one of the important sources of the diverse processes taking place in outer space. No absolute balance of these forces exists in the various areas of the Universe: one force always prevails over the other. Where repulsion predominates, matter and energy are dispersed and stars die. Where attraction predominates, matter and energy are concentrated and as a result new stars are born. Matter and energy thus move eternally in the Cosmos in the course of the conflict, interaction of these opposite forces.

We have pointed out earlier that opposite processes of assimilation and dissimilation are inherent in living organisms. It is their conflict, interaction that constitutes the specific source of development of everything living. These opposite processes cannot be in a state of absolute equilibrium; one of them must prevail. In a young organism assimilation gains ascendancy over dissimilation and determines its growth, development. When dissimilation prevails the organism grows old and deteriorates. In all organisms, however, young or old, these processes interact. It is their interaction, contradiction that makes up life. When this contradiction ends, life ceases.

Social development also proceeds on the basis of the unity and conflict of opposites. Contradictions in material production, especially between productive forces and relations of production, are particularly important among the contradictions of social development. In antagonistic class societies the contradiction between productive forces and relations of production is expressed in the conflict between hostile classes, which leads to social revolution, to replacement of the old social system by the new.

And so, objects and phenomena have opposite sides, they represent the unity of opposites. Opposites not merely exist side by side, but are in a state of constant contradiction, conflict between themselves. The conflict of opposites is the inner content, the source of development of reality.

Such is the essence of the dialectical law of the unity and conflict of opposites.

2. Diversity of Contradictions

A multitude of the most diverse contradictions exists in the world. We come up against them all the time in our daily life. They are taken up by various sciences. Marxist dialectics, as distinct from the other sciences, studies the most general contradictions. We shall examine internal and external, antagonistic and non-antagonistic, basic and nonbasic contradictions, these being large and important groups of contradictions.

Internal and External Contradictions

Marxist dialectics first of all differentiates between internal and external contradictions.

The interaction, the struggle of opposite sides of a *given* object make up its *internal contradictions.* The contradictory relations of a given object *to its environment,* to the objects of this environment are *its external contradictions.*

The opponents of Marxist dialectics distort the role of different groups of contradictions in development. They deny the decisive significance of internal contradictions and regard external contradictions as the sole source of development. From their viewpoint, for example, the source of development of class society is not the struggle of opposite classes, but the contradiction between society and nature. They do not want to understand that the relation of man to nature as such, and the degree of his domination over it, depend on class relations in society, on the character of the social system.

Both internal and external contradictions are inherent in objects and phenomena of the material world, but internal contradictions, contradictions within the object itself, are the principal, decisive ones in development. It is these contradictions that are the main source of development. Thus, Marxist dialectics regards motion as *self-motion* of matter, as *internal motion,* whose driving forces or impulses are contained within the developing objects and phenomena *themselves.*

The interaction, the struggle of wave and corpuscular properties of matter, the forces of attraction and repulsion, assimilation and dissimilation and other opposites, which we mentioned earlier as the sources of development in various spheres of reality, are not introduced into objects and phenomena from outside, but are inherent in them.

Internal contradictions are the source of development because they determine the appearance or nature of the object itself. If it were not for its internal contradictions, the object would not be what it is. An atom, for example, could not exist without the interaction, the "struggle" of the positively charged nucleus and negatively charged electrons; an organism could not exist without assimilation and dissimilation, and so on.

All outside influences exerted on an object are always refracted through its intrinsic contradictions, and this is also a manifestation of their determining role in development. Changes in the external environment merely give an inpulse to the development of organisms. But in what direction and to what ends development ultimately leads depends in the final account on the organism's metabolism, i.e., on the interaction of assimilation and dissimilation characteristic of this organism.

The source of social development also lies in society itself, in its intrinsic internal contradictions. But the direction in which a country develops and what social system it has depend on how its internal, class contradictions are resolved. Revolution is not made to order, it cannot be imposed on the people from without. It was internal contradictions— between the peasants and the feudal class, between the working class and the bourgeoisie, between the broad masses and imperialism—that led to the overthrow of the monarchy and precipitated national democratic revolution in Ethiopia.

It is true that there have been instances when the social system was imposed on a country by external reactionary forces. But regimes foisted on a people from outside are not stable and collapse at the first serious trial.

Although materialist dialectics emphasises the decisive role of internal contradictions, it does not deny the significance of external contradictions in development. Their role is diverse and they are very often a necessary requisite for development. Such, for example, is the contradiction between society and nature from which man has to win his material wealth.

External contradictions can facilitate development or impede it, lend it different shades or forms, but usually are unable to shape the main course of a process or of development as a whole. The victory of socialism in the Soviet Union, for example, was ensured by correctly resolving the internal contradictions, above all the antagonism between the proletariat and the bourgeoisie which had been overthrown but not yet fully liquidated. But the advance to socialism continued in spite of the external contradictions that existed between the Soviet state and the capitalist countries, which did everything in their power to restore the capitalist system in the USSR. Political boycott and economic blockade, foreign intervention in the early years of Soviet power, repeated military provocations and, lastly, the Nazi invasion greatly impeded the Soviet Union's development, but all these intrigues of imperialism could not halt the victorious advance of socialism.

Since internal contradictions determine the development of all objects and phenomena, it is especially necessary in practical activity to be able to bring to light and resolve these contradictions. At the same time it is essential not to neglect the external contradictions either, because they, too, are important in development.

Success cannot be achieved unless the interconnection, interaction of internal and external contradictions are taken into account.

Antagonistic and Non-Antagonistic Contradictions

When we speak of antagonistic and non-antagonistic contradictions we have in mind above all the sphere of social phenomena. It is true that there are antagonisms of a certain kind in living organisms—between certain types of bacteria, predatory and non-predatory animals, and between some plants—but they must not be confused with social antagonisms.

Antagonistic contradictions are above all contradictions between classes, whose interests are irreconcilably hostile. These are the most acute and obvious contradictions caused by the profoundly opposite conditions of life, by the aims and purposes of different classes. The main feature of these contradictions is that they cannot be resolved within the framework of the social system of which they are typical. As they grow deeper and more acute, these antagonistic contradictions lead to bitter clashes, to conflicts. A social revolution is the only means for resolving them.

The contradiction between the bourgeoisie and the proletariat is the most acute and profound contradiction in capitalist society. The antagonism between the bourgeoisie and the proletariat is a result of their objective positions in society. The bourgeoisie owns all the means of production and by virtue of this appropriates the lion's share of the material wealth produced by society. It dominates politically and enjoys everything that culture can give. The proletariat owns no means of production and hence is compelled to work for the bourgeoisie. It produces all the material wealth but receives only a negligible part of it. Its political rights are limited and it is frequently deprived of the possibility of benefiting from scientific and cultural achievements.

The interests of the bourgeoisie and the proletariat are diametrically opposite: the bourgeoisie seeks to perpetuate its rule, while the proletariat wants to emancipate itself from exploitation. As a result, a bitter class struggle goes on between them, which inevitably ends in the socialist revolution. The class struggle and the socialist revolution are thus special forms of resolving capitalism's antagonistic contradictions.

Bourgeois ideologists and revisionists deny the existence of class antagonisms in contemporary capitalist society. They call a bourgeois state a "welfare state", and assert that in a modern capitalist society there are no antagonistic classes and no class struggle. These fabrications are needed to slacken the vigilance of the working class and weaken its positions in the struggle against the bourgeoisie.

In reality, however, far from vanishing, these antagonistic contradictions of capitalism are growing more and more acute. They will remain as long as capitalism exists and will disappear only with the victory of socialism.

A distinguishing feature of the developing countries is the antagonistic contradiction between the counter-revolutionary front (the feudal class, and compradore and bureaucratic bourgeoisie), which is supported by imperialism, and the broad front of revolutionary forces that rests on the alliance of workers and peasants. A close ally of the revolutionary front is the petty bourgeoisie; other oppressed sections of society, and progressive and patriotic elements which have transcended the limits of their class also side with the revolutionary front.

This contradiction is solved when the resistance of the counter-revolutionary forces is crushed by the combined efforts of the revolutionary forces, the working class and the peasantry in the first place. The solution of this contradiction begins in the course of the national democratic revolution and is completed in the course of the socialist revolution.

Non-antagonistic contradictions are contradictions between those classes and social groups, whose fundamental interests coincide. These contradictions are gradually overcome and are not solved through a social revolution. Such, for example, are the contradictions between the working class and the peasants. Under capitalism the town exploits the country and, to a certain degree, the peasant extends his animosity for the town to the worker. The peasant owns property (land, draught animals, implements, etc.) and is interested in preserving it. The worker, on the other hand, has no property. The interests of the workers and peasants also clash in the market where the peasant tries to sell the products of his labour at the highest price possible. Taken together, all this makes for certain contradictions between the working class and the peasants under capitalism.

The interests of the workers and the peasants are contradictory in particular things, but in the fundamental thing they fully coincide: they are both exploited classes. That is why they strive to put an end to exploitation and in this fundamental question their interests are identical. This community of fundamental interests creates an objective basis for the alliance of the working class and the peasants in the struggle against the capitalist system.

The CPSU took into account the community of the vital interests of the workers and peasants, and united them in a mighty social force which defeated capitalism. Subsequently, in the course of socialist construction, the contradictions between the working class and the peasants, inherited from capitalism, were eliminated. Their unity in developed socialist society is becoming ever stronger and invincible.

The contradictions of socialist society, too, are of a non-antagonistic nature; this will be explained later in greater detail.

Basic and Non-Basic Contradictions

Objects and phenomena, from the simplest to the most complex, contain not one but several contradictions simultaneously.

To find our way in all these contradictions we must single out the basic, cardinal contradiction. The *basic contradiction* is that which plays the decisive, leading part in development and influences all other contradictions.

The basic, decisive contradiction of the chemical process, for example, is the contradiction between association and dissociation of atoms; of the biological process, the contradictory nature of metabolism, etc.

It is particularly important to find the basic contradiction of social life, which is exceptionally complex and many-sided. The discovery of this basic contradiction helps the advanced classes of society and the Marxist parties to elaborate the correct line of action and efficiently organise practical work.

A mass of contradictions is present in contemporary society. In any capitalist country there is the antagonism between the social character of the production process and the private form of appropriation, between labour and capital. There are contradictions between capitalist countries, between their groupings, blocs, and so on. Certain contradictions and differences exist between socialist countries.

Which is the basic, decisive contradiction in this multitude of contradictions in contemporary society?

The contradiction between the *forces of socialism,* as represented by the world socialist system, on the one hand, and the *reactionary forces of imperialism,* on the other, is the basic, decisive contradiction of contemporary society as a whole. It embodies two lines, two historical trends.

The contradiction between socialism and imperialism has a tremendous impact on the entire course of world history. It influences the struggle of classes in the capitalist countries themselves, the struggle of the peoples in the colonies and dependent countries against their oppressors and the contradictions between the imperialist countries themselves. The existence of the world socialist system is a great stumbling block to the imperialists and prevents them from unleashing another world war and from trampling upon the sovereign rights of other nations with impunity; it fires the hearts of working people in capitalist countries with confidence in the righteousness of their cause and lends them strength in their struggle against the exploiters. As the socialist system develops economically, politically and culturally, its influence in the world grows. That is why Marxist parties organise their practical work with account for the operation of this paramount contradiction of our age—the constant growth in the might of the socialist forces and the weakening of the imperialist and reactionary forces.

The basic contradiction of the present epoch, the contradiction between socialism and imperialism, does not remove the deep contradictions within the capitalist world.

The Final Document of the International Meeting of Communist and Workers' parties held in Moscow in June 1969 notes that contemporary conditions are characterised by the aggravation of the existing contradictions of capitalism and the rise of new ones. In the first place, they include the contradiction between the unusual opportunities afforded by the scientific and technical revolution and the obstacles to their exploitation in the interests of the whole of society which capitalism creates by using a large part of scientific achievements and enormous material resources for military purposes, thus squandering national wealth; the contradiction between the social character of modern production and the state-monopoly character of controlling it; the growing contradiction between labour and capital and also the deepening antagonism between the interests of the overwhelming majority of the nation and the financial oligarchy; the aggravation of the contradiction between the newly-free countries and imperialism, which endeavours to shackle them with the fetters of neocolonialism.

It is up to the Marxist parties to make the most of all the contradictions of capitalism and thus wage a successful struggle for peace, democracy, national liberation and socialism.

There are no hard and fast boundaries between internal and external, antagonistic and non-antagonistic, basic and non-basic contradictions. In reality they are intertwined, pass into one another and play a different part in development. That is why each contradiction should be approached separately, taking into account the conditions in which it manifests itself and the role it plays.

The Communist Party of the Soviet Union approaches the contradictions of social development concretely: it takes into account historical conditions, singles out the chief contradictions and employs the main forces and resources to resolve them. In the first years of Soviet power the contradiction between the advanced political system established in the country and the backward economy inherited from tsarist Russia made itself felt very strongly. This contradiction was solved in the process of industrialisation.

As industrialisation made headway, the contradiction between socialist industry and small-scale peasant farming became more and more acute. This contradiction, too, was solved by the efforts of the people and the Party through the organisation of the peasants in collective farms. The elimination of these contradictions was of decisive significance in building socialism in the Soviet Union.

3. Contradictions of Socialist Society and Ways of Eliminating Them

The victory of socialism in the Soviet Union resulted in the abolition of the exploiting classes and of the causes that give rise to the exploitation of man by man, in the elimination of the antithesis between town and country, between manual and mental labour. The community of fundamental interests of the workers, peasants and the intelligentsia formed the basis for the socio-political and ideological unity of the Soviet people. Friendship among the many Soviet peoples struck firm root and grew stronger. As the USSR advances to communism this unity is further strengthened, the nations and social groups draw closer together, they enrich each other and the distinctions between them gradually disappear. This, however, does not mean that there are no contradictions under socialism. Socialist society develops continuously and where there is development there always exists the old and the new and, consequently, struggle between them. "Antagonism and contradiction," Lenin wrote, "are not one and the same thing. Under socialism the first will vanish, the second will remain."*

Lenin pointed not only to the existence of contradictions under socialism, but also disclosed their major distinction, their *non-antagonistic character*. This is because there are no hostile classes and no exploitat⁻

---

* *Lenin Miscellany XI*, Russ. ed., Moscow, 1931, p. 357.

in socialist society where public ownership of the means of production unites the people. The contradictions of socialist society are contradictions and difficulties of growth connected with the rapid advance of the socialist economy and the rise in the material and cultural requirements of the people. These are contradictions between the new and the old, the progressive and the backward.

The contradictions of socialist society are overcome by the common effort of all the working people led by the Communist Party and the Soviet Government. The Party's correct, scientifically substantiated policy, the unity of the party and the people, the full support given by the people to steps taken by the Party and the Government ensure the timely disclosure and elimination of contradictions. That is why contradictions of socialism do not turn into conflicts, do not assume the character of social upheavals. Under capitalism the solution of contradictions leads to its doom, while the elimination of socialism's contradictions actually strengthens the socialist system and facilitates the country's advance.

In socialist society production relations correspond to the nature of productive forces inasmuch as the social nature of productive forces corresponds to social ownership of the means of production and social forms of distribution. Means of life are distributed not depending on capital possessed, but in accordance with the quantity and quality of work done. This correspondence between productive forces and production relations, however, does not preclude the existence of certain contradictions between them.

Production relations under socialism are a chain of economic interaction of people whose separate links do not always manage to keep abreast of the growth of the productive forces and thus become obsolete. As a result they enter into a contradiction with the productive forces and may arrest economic development.

The Communist Party and the Soviet state continuously improve socialist production relations, replace their old links with new, advanced ones, and in this way overcome the contradictions of socialist production. Here is an example. In the period when the mechanisation of agriculture in the Soviet Union was still low, small agricultural production co-operatives with relatively small cultivated areas were set up. Later the level of mechanisation of agriculture increased immensely, but owing to small size of the co-operatives it was impossible to effectively employ farm machinery. This gave rise to certain contradictions in agricultural production. But they were solved by means of enlarging the co-operatives, and agricultural production increased.

The development of socialist society is accompanied by the rise and solution of contradictions between the new dimensions and objectives of the national economy, the new tasks which confront society, and the mechanism of management, the forms and methods of running the economy and administering society in general. The Party and the socialist state solve this contradiction by keeping on improving the economic mechanism and the entire system of administration.

The vast majority of the Soviet people actively participate in building communism, but there are individuals who still cling to the old, obsolete methods of production, to backward technology, etc. There are also those whose minds are infected with survivals of capitalism. The interests and actions of these individuals run counter to the interests of society. These individuals are re-educated by the efforts of the people and the Communist Party, while penalties are imposed on the more incorrigible ones.

It should be stressed that contradictions between the vast majority of Soviet people and individuals who carry survivals of the old do not stem from the nature of the socialist system but from the legacy and influence of capitalism from shortcomings in ideological work, education, etc. These contradictions are temporary and undoubtedly will be fully eliminated.

How are the contradictions of socialism brought to light and solved?

The method of disclosing the contradictions of socialist society lies in *criticism* and *self-criticism*. But, having brought to light contradictions, the method of criticism and self-criticism by itself is unable to resolve them. Their solution depends on the labour efforts of the entire nation and the competent organisational and educational work both of the Party and the Government. Constant development and improvement of production, active participation of the people in communist construction, the painstaking and multifarious work of the party in educating the Soviet citizen—such are the main means of eliminating contradictions of socialist society.

Besides internal contradictions, the Soviet Union and the entire world socialist community are in antagonistic contradiction with the world capitalist system. Although this contradiction is external, it considerably affects the country's development and it must not be underestimated. The CPSU and the Soviet Government are doing all they can to solve this contradiction in a peaceful way, on the basis of peaceful coexistence of states with different social systems. A world thermonuclear war would result in colossal loss of human life and destruction and greatly retard mankind's progress. That is why the strnggle to prevent another world war and to preserve universal peace is the overriding duty of all honest people.

Struggle for peace is an essential requisite of social progress and of the successful building of socialism and communism.

The Law of Passage of Quantitative into Qualitative Changes

The law of the passage of quantitative into qualitative changes shows *how, in what way* development proceeds and *what is the mechanism* of this process.

To understand the essence of this law we should first of all understand quality and quantity.

1. Quality and Quantity

We are surrounded by very many of the most diverse objects and phenomena and all of them are in a state of constant motion or change. Nevertheless, we do not confuse these objects, but differentiate between them and define them. They do not merge into some kind of grey mass; each one differs from the others by certain specific properties of its own.

Let us take, for example, such a metal as gold. It has a characteristic yellow colour, ductility and malleability, a definite density and heat capacity, melting and boiling points. Gold dissolves neither in alkali nor in many acids; it is not very active chemically and does not oxidise. All this taken together sets gold apart from other metals.

All that which makes an object what it is, what distinguishes it from innumerable other objects, is its *quality*.

All objects and phenomena possess quality. It is this that enables us to define and distinguish them. What, for example, sets living matter apart from non-living matter? The ability to enter into metabolic interchange with the environment, purposively to respond to external influences, to propagate. These and certain other properties make up the quality of living matter.

Social phenomena, too, differ qualitatively. The dominance of commodity production, the existence of capitalist property, wage labour and other features distinguish capitalism from feudalism. For instance, thousands of peasant associations, each uniting a definite number of peasants, have been set up in some socialist-oriented countries. But such an association is not simply a sum total of its members, but a new quality. It is a peasant union, the beginning of their collective life and new relations between them, relations of mutual assistance and cooperation.

Quality is manifested in properties. A *property* characterises a thing from one side only, whereas quality gives the general idea of an object as a whole. Yellow colour, malleability, ductility and other features of gold taken separately are its properties, while taken together they constitute its quality.

Besides a definite quality all objects possess *quantity*. As distinct from quality, quantity reflects the *degree* of development or *intensity* of an object's intrinsic properties and also its size, volume, etc. Quantity is usually expressed by a *number*. Size, weight, volume of objects, the intensity of their intrinsic colours, of the sounds they emit, etc., are expressed numerically.

Social phenomena also have quantitative characteristics. Each socioeconomic system has a corresponding level or degree of development of production. Any country possesses a definite productive capacity, labour, raw material and power resources.

Quantity and quality are a *unity* inasmuch as they represent the two sides of one and the same object. But there are also important distinctions between them. A change in quality leads to a change of the object, to its conversion into another object; on the other hand, a change in quantity within certain limits does not bring about a noticeable transformation of the object. If capitalist property, i.e., the most important qualitative feature of capitalism, is abolished and socialist property is substituted for it, a new, qualitatively different system, socialism, will supersede capitalism. But if capitalist property is enlarged, centralised, concentrated in the hands of a small group of monopolists or of the bourgeois state, as is the case in the capitalist world today, capitalism will not cease to be capitalism.

The unity of quantity and quality is called *measure*. Measure is a kind of boundary, a framework within which the object remains what it is. A "disturbance" of this measure, of this definite combination of quantitative and qualitative sides, leads to a change in the object, its conversion into another object. For example, the measure for mercury in liquid state is the temperature from -39°C to + 357°C. At -39°C mercury solidifies, while at + 357°C it begins to boil and becomes vapourised.

Quantitative and qualitative definiteness is inherent in social phenomena as well.

Capitalism and socialism, being qualitatively unlike social systems, have their own quantitative distinctions that reflect the dynamics and the level of development, indicators of the state of phenomena and aspects (productive forces, economic growth rates, labour resources, population, education, social maintenance, subsistence minimum, occupational injuries, crime, free time, etc.), correlation, proportions of the economic subdivisions and branches (accumulation and consumption, industrial and agricultural production, etc.), Here it is also necessary to reckon with the fact that a range of quantitative features are intrinsic either to socialism or to capitalism in view of the contrasting aims of production under these social systems and the specifics of their economies.

It should also be stressed that a planned and balanced transformation of quantitative and qualitative features of various sides of the life of society is typical of socialism.

In both cognition and practice it is very important to take into account the unity of the quantitative and qualitative sides of phenomena.

2. The Passage of Quantitative into Qualitative Changes—A Law of Development

We pointed out earlier that a change in quantity within certain limits does not lead to a change in the qualitative state of an object. But as soon as these limits are overstepped and the "measure" is upset, the seemingly inessential quantitative changes inevitably bring about a radical qualitative transformation: quantity passes into quality. In the process of development, Marx wrote, "merely quantitative differences beyond a certain point pass into qualitative changes".*

The passage of quantitative into qualitative changes is a *universal law* of development of the material world.

Moreover, development itself is, above all, a conversion of quantitative changes into qualitative ones, inasmuch as the movement of objects and phenomena from the lower to the higher, from the old to the new takes place in the course of this conversion.

In order to reveal the universal character of this law let us see how it operates in different spheres of reality.

Modern physics has proved that some elementary particles can be transmuted into other, qualitatively different ones. The process of their transmutation is always connected with a certain quantitative accumulation: it takes place only if the particles possess a certain, sufficiently high level of energy.

The numerous changes of substances from one state to another (from solid to liquid, from liquid to gas, etc.) are also manifestations of the law of the passage of quantitative into qualitative changes. When water, for example, is heated above 100°C it is transformed into a different quality, steam. The properties of steam are distinct from those of water. Salts and sugar, for example, do not dissolve in steam whereas they do in water.

* Karl Marx, *Capital*, Vol. I, p. 292.

The law of the passage of quantitative into qualitative changes is strikingly apparent in chemical processes. Mendeleyev's periodic law shows that the quality of chemical elements depends on the quantity of the positive charge of their atomic nucleus. Within certain limits a quantitative change in the charge causes no qualitative changes in the chemical element, but at a definite stage these quantitative changes lead to the formation of a new element. Thus, during radioactive disintegration, as the uranium nucleus loses atomic weight and charge, it is ultimately transmuted into a qualitatively new element, lead.

In general, chemistry is the science that studies qualitative transformations of substances resulting from quantitative changes. A molecule of oxygen, for example, contains two atoms, but as soon as one more atom of oxygen is added it becomes ozone, a qualitatively new chemical substance.

In the organic world, too, quantitative changes pass into qualitative ones. One can daily perceive the dependence of the changes in quality on quantitative accumulations by observing the cyclical development of plants and animals whose passage from one stage into another takes place in keeping with the laws of the biological rhythm which has strict chronological limits and is caused by changes in the quantity of light, heat, moisture, etc. Under the influence of a certain amount of moisture and heat, a seed turns into a stalk; but a different quantitative proportion of these natural components is needed for an ear to emerge and mature. A chicklet or a nestling will develop and hatch from an egg only if the latter receives a definite quantity of heat of a certain temperature and over a definite quantity of time (knowledge of these quantitative proportions is applied in incubators which replace a sitting hen).

The passage of quantitative into qualitative changes takes place in social development as well. Thus, the transition from capitalism to socialism, effected by the socialist revolution, has definite quantitative prerequisites: growth of the productive forces under capitalism, growth of the social character of production, and an increase in the number of revolutionary proletariat, etc.

In objective reality we witness not only the development of quantitative changes into qualitative ones, but also the reverse process of an increase in quantity under the influence of qualitative changes. The radical qualitative change in the social system, the replacement of capitalism by socialism, entails a substantial change in various quantities: increase in the volume of industrial and agricultural output, more rapid rates of economic and cultural development, growth of the national income, the wellbeing of the people, etc.

Quantitative and qualitative changes are thus interconnected and influence each other.

The Unity of Continuity and Discontinuity (Leap) in Development

Quantitative changes are relatively slow and continuous, while qualitative transformations are discontinuous, leaplike. Development therefore appears as the unity of two differing but interconnected forms or stages— *continuity* and *discontinuity (leap).* *

Continuity in development is the stage of slow, imperceptible *quantitative* accumulation. It does not affect the quality of an object, but introduces insignificant quantitative changes in it; it is a process of increasing or of decreasing what exists.

Discontinuity, or *leap,* is a stage of radical *qualitative* change in an object, a moment or period when the old quality passes into a new one. In contrast to the concealed, slow quantitative changes, a leap is a more or less open, relatively swift change in the *quality* of an object. This change occurs in a relatively rapid manner, even when the qualitative transformations assume the form of a gradual transition.

Leaps in the development of the material world may be: formation of some elementary particles from others, a change in the state of a substance, the birth of a new chemical element, or a previously non-existent species of plant or animal, of a new social system, etc. Each one of them results from definite quantitative accumulation.

Since a leap results in destruction of the old and development of what is new and progressive, leaps are of tremendous importance in development.

Leaps are particularly significant in the development of society, where they often acquire the nature of social revolutions abolishing the old and establishing a new social system, thereby removing obstacles to social progress. Such a leap is national democratic revolution, currently under way in some socialist-oriented states. It has put an end to the monarchy where it existed, to the archaic, autocratic monarchical rule, and nationalised the land, industry and insurance companies. These and other revolutionary measures are designed to set up a new society—a people's democratic republic led by the party of the working class.

---

* Continuity and discontinuity are inherent not only in the development, but also in the *state* of matter. Matter, as we know, has wave (continuous) and corpuscular (discontinuous) properties.

Since development always appears as a unity of quantitative (continuous) and qualitative (leap-like) changes, in practice and in cognition it is necessary to take both these stages of development into account. To ignore any one of them means to distort the process of development, to lapse into metaphysics.

It is most typical of metaphysicians to deny that qualitative changes take place, and to reduce development to imperceptible quantitative accumulation. The theory of *preformation* is an example of such understanding of development in the field of biology. The proponents of this theory maintain that the embryo is a fully developed, mature organism, but on a microscopic scale. Development of the organism, from their point of view, is simple growth, an increase in the embryo's size. In reality, however, the embryo undergoes deep qualitative changes in the course of its development.

Bourgeois ideologists follow this metaphysical line of thought in seeking to explain social development. They understand social development as pure continuity without leaps or revolutions. By doing so they deny the need for a socialist revolution and try to perpetuate the capitalist system.

The metaphysical denial of leaps in social development is inherent in revisionism. Just as bourgeois ideologists, revisionists deny the need of qualitative changes in society. They oppose the Marxist-Leninist theory of socialist revolution with the idea of the gradual transformation of capitalism into socialism. By doing so they divert the working class from revolutionary struggle, which can bring about socialist change.

It is similarly wrong to ignore quantitative changes, to reduce development merely to leaps, to a break in continuity, as was done, for example, by the French 19th-century scientist Georges Cuvier. He claimed that some kind of catastrophes occurred on Earth one after another, as a result of which old species of plants and animals were fully replaced by new ones. Moreover, Cuvier denied any connection between the new and the vanished species.

Denial of quantitative changes serves as the theoretical basis of *anarchism,* a petty-bourgeois trend hostile to Marxism. Anarchists scoff at the prolonged, painstaking work to accumulate forces, organise the people and gradually prepare them for revolutionary action. Recklessness and conspiratorial activities are typical anarchist tactics which have seriously harmed the working-class movement.

Marxist dialectics demands a competent analysis of continuous and leap-like forms of development, particularly of their unity in social development. Since a leap or revolution is decisive in the development of society, the transition from capitalism to socialism can be effected neither through slow, quantitative changes nor through reforms, but only through a qualitative transformation of the capitalist system, through a socialist revolution.

The CPSU is a consistently revolutionary party. This is borne out by its heroic history. From the very outset it embarked on the course of effecting a revolutionary transformation of society and undeviatingly pursued it by leading the struggle of the working people for the destruction of capitalism and the victory of the qualitatively new, socialist, system.

But a revolution cannot win if it is not thoroughly prepared. Therefore, the party painstakingly raised the class army of the revolution, assembled forces and created the necessary conditions for the revolution. A brilliant example of this is the preparation for, and the consummation of, the Great October Socialist Revolution. Working in extremely difficult conditions of tsarist rule the party organised and ideologically tempered the workers, accumulated forces and gained influence among the broad sections of the working people. And when the conditions for revolutionary action became ripe it boldly led the working class and its allies into an assault against capitalism, along the road of the revolutionary reorganisation of society.

And so, *quantitative and qualitative definiteness, quantity and quality are inherent in all objects and phenomena. Quantity and quality are interconnected; in the process of development imperceptible, gradual quantitative changes pass into basic, qualitative changes. This passage takes the form of a leap.*

This is the essence of the dialectical law of the passage of quantitative into qualitative changes.

A leap is a universal, indispensable form by which quantitative changes pass into qualitative changes. Since, however, the most diverse objects and phenomena exist in the world, leaps too are diverse. Let us examine this question in greater detail.

3. Diversity of Forms of the Passage from the Old Quality to the New

The basic feature of any leap is a radical turn in development or formation of a new quality. But in different objects this turn, the passage from the old quality to the new, takes place differently, in various forms. The form of the leap indicates *how, in what way* the transition from the old to the new takes place—swiftly, completely, at once or gradually, in stages. Some leaps are *sudden* and *swift*, with the old quality passing into the new completely and at once.

Other leaps are less rapid and not so sudden. In this case the old quality does not pass into the new at once and completely, but in stages: the elements of the old *gradually* wither away and are replaced by elements of the new quality just as gradually. A leap of this kind, as a gradual *qualitative* change, must not be confused with a gradual *quantitative* accumulation. For all its graduality this leap too is a much faster and more noticeable change than the most intensive change of quantity. Moreover gradual quantitative changes do not affect the essence, the nature of an object, whereas every leap, even a gradual one, is always a decisive turn in development, it transforms the object and turns it into a qualitatively new object.

On what does the form of a leap depend?

First of all it depends on the *character* of the phenomenon undergoing development. Each phenomenon passes into another, a new one, in its own particular way. For example, the transmutation of certain elementary particles into others takes place through an explosion. As soon as an electron and positron clash at sufficiently high energies, a flash (explosion) occurs instantly, testifying to the transmutation of the original particles into others (photons). The transmutation of certain chemical elements into others during an increase or decrease in the charge of the atomic nuclei is just as instantaneous.

In organic nature leaps as a rule are of a gradual character. The birth of new species usually depends on the environment. The environment, however, changes slowly, gradually, This largely explains why new species of plants and animals do not arise at once, but in the process of a long development, in the course of which organisms gradually acquire and pass on by heredity new characteristics which conform to the changed environment, and lose the old characteristics which no longer correspond to the new conditions.

Man too, as we know, arose not at once but in the course of evolution. Notwithstanding the gradual character of transformation of the anthropoid ape into a man, the transformation as such was the greatest leap, turning point,in the development of the animal world. It marked the emergence and development of human society.

The form of a leap depends on the *conditions* in which the phenomenon develops. During radioactive disintegration, for example, the nuclei of some chemical elements are transmuted into nuclei of other, lighter elements, and this process is accompanied by the conversion of atomic energy into thermal energy. This conversion, depending on the conditions, may assume the form of an explosion (in an atomic bomb) or the gradual conversion of atomic energy into heat (in reactors of atomic power plants).

In social development transition from the old quality to the new may take the form of rapid and violent changes or gradual changes.

The 1917 October Socialist Revolution in Russia, the greatest qualitative turning point in history which ushered in a new era in the development of mankind, the era of socialism and communism, was a rapid and violent leap. As a result of this armed uprising the Russian proletariat in alliance with the peasants put an end to the political rule of the bourgeoisie by a single blow, and came to power.

The cultural revolution in the Soviet Union was also a leap, a revolutionary transition to a new, socialist culture; it was effected, however, not at once, but gradually, in step with the successes of socialist construction, which creates conditions for a radical improvement of public education and political education of the masses and the rise of a new, socialist intelligentsia.

It is very important to take into account the distinctive features of leaps in practice. Without ascertaining these distinctive features it is impossible to find the correct ways for a transition from the old to the new.

The question of the forms of transition from capitalism to socialism in different countries is particularly important at present. The transition to socialism in any country can be effected only through a socialist revolution. Without a qualitative leap, without a revolution, transition to socialism is impossible. But the concrete ways in which the revolution will proceed in each individual country depend on the level of the country's development, the strength and organisation of the working class and its allies, the traditions and customs of the people, the strength and the resistance of the bourgeoisie, and a number of other internal and external factors.

The experience of building socialism in the Soviet Union and the other socialist countries shows that the development of the socialist revolution in various countries cannot be the same and that in the future, forms of development will be ever more diverse.

The national democratic revolution in Ethiopia is following a course of its own. In view of the country's backwardness, the existence of the survivals and mainstays of feudalism, and the smallness of the working class and its inadequate organisation, the progressive part of the army became the main revolutionary force. It is important to note that the people of Ethiopia had to take up arms in order to protect the gains of the revolution and the country's territorial integrity against internal and external reaction.

4. The Nature of Qualitative Changes During the Transition from Socialism to Communism

Communist society passes through two phases in its development—socialism and communism.

Socialism and communism are two stages of *one and the same* socio-economic formation, stages differing in the degree of economic development and maturity of social relations. They have a common economic foundation in the public ownership of the means of production, and, consequently, have relations of cooperation and mutual assistance among people and a single communist ideology. The law of planned, proportionate development of society operates both under socialism and under communism. The aim of social production (to fully satisfy the material and cultural requirements of the working people), and the ways for achieving this aim (the constant development and improvement of production on the basis of advanced technology) are also identical under socialism and communism.

At the same time there are qualitative distinctions between socialism and communism. Communism is the higher stage of the communist socio-economic formation. Under communism, mechanisation and automation will be exceptionally high. The level of production will be high enough to enable society to change from the socialist principle of distribution: "From each according to his ability, to each according to his work", to the qualitatively new, communist principle: "From each according to his ability, to each according to his needs." The nature of labour too will be greatly altered. All members of society will develop an inner urge to work for the common good voluntarily and in accordance with their abilities.

With the victory of communism important qualitative changes will take place not only in the economy, but also in social relations, the way of life and consciousness of people. Essential distinctions between town and country will disappear and then distinctions between manual and mental labour will be obliterated: all citizens in the country will become workers of communist society. Under communism the state will wither away and the socialist state will develop into communist public self-government.

Such deep-going qualitative transformations take time, but above all they depend on definite material, political and spiritual prerequisites: a highly developed material and technical basis, perfect social relations between people who know no exploitation, a rich culture and a high level of awareness of the people. Since all these conditions can be created only in the course of socialist constrnction, it is impossible to perform a leap from capitalism directly into the highest stage of communism. Lenin wrote: "From capitalism mankind can pass directly only to socialism, i.e., to the social onwership of the means of production and the distribution of products according to the amount of work performed by each individual."*

Communism *naturally* and *necessarily* grows out of established, mature socialism and develops on the basis of its great economic and cultural achievements. Already today a developed socialist society has tangible and visible features of communism. Communist forms of labour, organisation of production and public forms of satisfying the material and cultural needs of the people are rapidly developing. These communist features will continue to develop and improve.

The transition to communism takes place on the basis of the preservation and improvement of the achievements of socialist economy and culture. That is why it is a gradual, phased process, and not a sudden leap. "Socialism," Lenin wrote, "must inevitably evolve gradually into communism."**

For instance, the transition to the communist principle of distribution will take place in stages and not at once. At first the wellbeing of the people will rise to a level that will enable *all* members of society to live in easy circumstances. Later, when the material and technical basis of communism is built, there will be an abundance of material values for the whole population and society will come close to applying the principle of distribution according to requirements.

The gradual development of the socialist principle of distribution into the communist principle takes place on the basis of the development and improvement of distribution according to work in combination with the growth of public funds distributed free among all members of society. A considerable part of the material and cultural benefits is already distributed through the public funds, including state expenditure on education, public health, culture, sport, etc. In the future, as the material and technical basis of communism is built up, this form of distribution will steadily develop and gradually take the place of the socialist principle of distribution according to work done.

Moral stimuli, which are already part and parcel of the labour of a Soviet citizen, will gradually prevail. The transfer of the functions of state administration to public organisations and the remoulding of the mentality and way of life will not take place at once either.

---

* V.I. Lenin, "The Tasks of the Proletariat in Our Revolution", *Collected Works*, Vol. 24, pp. 84-85.
** Ibid., p. 85

The transition from socialism to communism is thus a process of improvement and development of socialist social relations, the gradual withering away of old and the birth of new forms of life, their intertwining and interdependence. This gradual transition is incompatible with undue haste, with the premature application of the principles of communism. The new forms of economic development, social organisation and way of life will strike root consecutively, step by step, as the material and spiritual prerequisites mature.

The gradual character of the transition to communism is governed by laws and determined by the very nature of the socialist system. Under socialism there are no classes opposed to society's advance to communism. The conscious planned activity of the CPSU and the Soviet state ensures the timely disclosure and elimination of contradictions arising in the course of this advance. This precludes social upheavals and sudden changes in the life of society; development becomes gradual and takes place without recessions which are so typical of capitalist society.

The Law of Negation of the Negation

The law of negation of the negation reveals the *general direction, tendency* of development of the material world.

In order to grasp the essence and significance of this law we must first of all ascertain what is *dialectical negation* and what place it holds in development.

1. Dialectical Negation and Its Role in Development

The passing away of the old which has outlived its age and the rise of the new and advanced proceeds constantly in every sphere. It is the replacement of the old by the new, of the dying by the emerging that constitutes development, while the overcoming of the old by the new, arising from the old, is called *negation*.

The term "negation" was introduced in philosophy by Hegel, but he invested it with an idealist meaning. From his point of view, negation was inherent in the development of the idea, of thought.

Marx and Engels preserved the term "negation" but interpreted it in a materialist way. They demonstrated that negation is an integral part of development of reality itself. "In no sphere can one undergo a development without negating one's previous mode of existence,"* Marx wrote.

The development of the Earth's crust, for example, has passed through a number of geological eras; each new era, arising on the basis of the preceding one, represents a certain negation of the old. In the organic world, too, each new species of plant or animal, arising on the basis of the old, at the same time represents its negation. The history of society also consists of a chain of negations of the old social order by the new: primitive-communal by slave-owning society; slave-owning society by feudalism; feudalism by capitalism; capitalism by socialism. Negation is also inherent in the development of knowledge and science. Each new, improved scientific theory negates the old, less developed.

Negation is not something introduced into an object or phenomenon from outside, but is the result of the object's or phenomenon's own, internal development. Objects and phenomena are contradictory and develop on the basis of their internal opposites; they themselves create the conditions for their destruction, for the passage into a new, higher quality. Negation is the overcoming of the old through internal contradictions, a result of self-development, self-movement of objects and phenomena. Thus, socialism comes to take the place of capitalism because it resolves the internal, intrinsic contradictions of the capitalist system. As they grow deeper and more acute, these contradictions find their solution in a socialist revolution.

National democratic revolutions in socialist-oriented states are also a negation—negation of the monarchy, of the semi-capitalist society.

Dialectical and Metaphysical Understanding of Negation

Dialectics and metaphysics differ in their understanding of the essence of negation. Misinterpreting the process of the development of the material reality, metaphysics regards negation as the casting aside, the absolute destruction of the old. Lenin called such an understanding of negation "empty" and "futile", because it precludes any possibility of further development.

That is how negation was understood by supporters of petty-bourgeois trends which existed in the early years of Soviet power. They advocated the view that the culture that had arisen under the bourgeois system should be discarded and a new, proletarian culture should be created from scratch.

* Karl Marx, "Moralising Criticism and Critical Morality", in: Karl Marx, Frederick Engels, *Collected Works,* Vol. 6, Moscow, 1976, p. 317.

Such conception of negation, far from promoting development, did irreparable harm. That is why, in criticising such views, the Communist Party and Lenin pointed to the need for making use of the cultural heritage of the past, maintaining that only by critically assimilating this heritage was it possible to create a genuinely proletarian, socialist culture.

Marxist dialectics reveals the true essence of dialectical negation. What is characteristic of Marxist dialectics, is not "empty", "futile" negation, but negation as a moment of connection, as a moment of development, retaining the positive.

In its interpretation of negation, dialectics proceeds from the premise that the new does not completely obliterate the old, but retains the best in it; in fact it not only retains it, but assimilates it and raises it to a new, higher level. Thus, when higher organisms negate the lower ones on whose basis they arose, they preserve the intrinsic cellular structure of the lower organisms, their selective nature of reflection and other featunes. A new social system, negating the old, preserves its productive forces, achievements of science, technology and culture. The connection of the new and the old likewise exists in knowledge, in science.

Thus, recognition of *continuity,* the connection of the new and the old in development, is a feature of the Marxist understanding of negation. But we must bear in mind that the new never takes over the old completely, as it is. It takes from the old only certain elements or aspects; moreover, it does not absorb them mechanically, but assimilates and transforms them in conformity with its own nature. Marxist dialectics calls for a critical attitude to the past experience of mankind, creative application of this experience and the strict account of the changed conditions and the new tasks of revolutionary practice. Marxist philosophy, for example, did not simply accept the progressive ideas of previous philosophies, but critically reworked and enriched them with the new achievements of science and practice, and raised philosophy as a science to a qualitatively new, higher stage.

The working class with its Marxist party is the most careful custodian of the finest achievements of the past. Upon coming to power the proletariat not only skillfully draws on all the achievements of the past epochs, but makes great progress in all areas of the economy, science and culture as it builds a new society.

2. The Progressive Nature of Development

Development as Progress

And so, we have ascertained that as a result of negation one or another contradiction is solved, the old is destroyed and the new arises. But does this bring development to an end? No, the rise of the new does not stop development. Anything new does not remain new for ever. While developing, it prepares the prerequisites for the rise of something newer and more progressive. And when these prerequisites and conditions ripen, negation again occurs. This is a *negation of the negation,* i.e., the negation of that which itself previously overcame the old; this is replacement of the new by something newer. The result of this second negation is again negated, overcome, and so on, *ad infinitum.* Development thus appears as a countless number of successive negations, as an endless replacement or overcoming of the old by the new.

Since each higher stage of development only negates what has become obsolete in the lower and at the same time accepts and augments the achievements of preceding stages, development as a whole becomes *progressive.* Progress is the general direction that is typical of dialectical developmentt.

Progress takes place in all spheres of reality. Let us outline the progressive development on our planet.

We have said that gas-dust matter containing the simplest chemical substances was the primary material from which the planets of the solar system, including the Earth, were formed. In the course of nature's development these substances became more and more complex. As a result living, organic nature arose. Living organisms also developed from the simple to the complex: from pre-cellular forms to the cell, from unicellular to multicellular and then to more complex animals, whose evolution led to the appearance of anthropoid beings and later to the appearance of man. With the rise of man the process of social development began. The consecutive stages in the progressive development of society were: primitive-communal, slave-owning, feudal, capitalist, and socialist systems.

Constant acceleration of the rate of development is a primary distinction of the progress of society. The process of man's development began approximately a million years ago. Since the history of contemporary man is limited to tens of thousands of years, we can imagine how slow the process of man's emergence was. Progress in the slave-owning and feudal societies was faster, although it, too, dragged out for millenniums. Capitalism develops much faster than feudalism. With the transition to socialism, the rate of economic and cultural growth has been tremendoulsy accelerated. When communism triumphs throughout the world, when mankind gets rid of capitalist relations retarding progress and gains the opportunity to concentrate all efforts on improvement of the conditions of life and the development of man, this growth will proceed at an unprecedented pace.

The Spiral-Like Character of Development

The progressive character of development is the principal but not the only feature of the law of negation of the negation. This law describes development not as movement along a straight line, but as an extremely complicated, *spiral-like* process, with a definite *repetition* of stages already passed, a certain return to the past. "A development that repeats, as it were, stages that have already been passed, but repeats them in a different way, on a higher basis ('the negation of negation'), a development, so to speak, that proceeds in spirals, not in a straight line."*

The spiral-like character of development may be seen in various spheres.

Mendeleyev's periodic law is perhaps one of its most striking manifestations in inorganic nature.

In the periodic table chemical elements are arranged according to the magnitude of the positive charge of their atomic nucleus. They form periods and series in which we observe a certain repetition of properties. Let us take, for example, the second period beginning with lithium. Lithium is an element with certain pronounced metallic properties, it is an alkali metal. As the charge of the nucleus in the elements following lithium grows, the properties characteristic of metals diminish and the non-metallic properties gradually increase. At the end of the period we find a typical metalloid (non-metal) fluorine and the inert gas neon. The next, third period again begins with an alkali metal (sodium) and ends with the non-metallic chlorine and the inert gas argon. The same is repeated in the subsequent periods where the metallic properties are negated by the non-metallic, and then in the following period the latter are again negated by the metallic properties. A seeming return to the old, the negation of negation, takes place.

This system of elements can be roughly pictured as an ascending, unwinding spiral. A repetition of the properties occurs at increasing intervals (two elements in the first period, eight in the second period, and

---

* V.I. Lenin, "Karl Marx", *Collected Works*, Vol. 21, p. 54.

so on), and it proceeds on a qualitatively different basis at each stage: the elements of each new period have a bigger nuclear charge, a more complex structure and new properties.

Spiral-like development occurs in the organic world as an well. Engels illustrated the operation of this law by referring to the development of a grain of barley. From a grain, landing in favourable conditions, there grows a stalk; this represents a negation of the grain. Then, an ear with new grains grows on the stalk; the new grains are a negation of the stalk—the negation of the negation. At the same time there is a certain return to the starting point, the grain, but on a new basis. The new grains differ from the original grain not only quantitatively (10-20 instead of 1) but often also in terms of their properties. Here development proceeds in the form of a spiral. It begins with a single grain from which several grow, and these in turn give rise to an even larger number, and so on.

Spiral-like development also takes place in social life. The primitive-communal system was the first form of social organisation. It was a classless society based on common ownership of the extremely primitive tools. Further development of production led to the negation of this system by the class, slave-owning society. The slave-owning system gave way to feudalism which in turn was negated by capitalism. In place of capitalism has come socialism, the first stage of communism. This is also a certain negation of the negation, a return to the initial point of development in a certain sense, but on an entirely different, qualitatively new basis.

Negation of the negation means a certain periodicity, recurrence in the progressive development of matter. But we should stress that a repetition of past stages of development is not an actual return to the old, but a rise of the new which often bears only an outward, formal resemblance to the old and has a totally different essence. Sodium which opens the third period in Mendeleyev's Table belongs, like lithium, to the group of alkali metals, but it has a more complex structure and its own intrinsic properties.

Social property prevailing under socialism reproduces, in a certain sense, the communal property of primitive society, but reproduces it on an entirely new material and spiritual basis, which can in no way be compared with the primitive communal system.

And so, *development occurs through the negation of the old by the new, the lower by the higher. Since the new, negating the old, retains and develops its positive features, development acquires a progressive character. At the same time development proceeds along a spiral, with repetition at higher stages of certain aspects and features of the lower stages.*

Such is the essence of the dialectical law of negation of the negation.

3. How the Law of Negation of the Negation
Operates Under Socialism

The law of negation of the negation operates in socialist society as well, but in a specific way.

The dominance of socialist property, the absence of antagonistic classes, the socio-political and ideological unity of the Soviet people fully preclude such forms of negation in Soviet society as social revolution, class battles and sudden political explosions characteristic of antagonistic class societies.

Under socialism the old is negated when it becomes clear that it no longer corresponds to the new conditions and tasks, when the objective prerequisites for its overcoming mature. The Soviet people, led by the Communist party and the Soviet Government, replace the old, that which hinders progress, by the new. In the Soviet Union there is a continuous process of supplanting obsolescent machinery by new, more improved, of replacing old forms of organisation of production and economic management by new forms, etc. The negation of the old and obsolete reinforces the economic, political and ideological mainstays of socialist society and is one of the important factors of its progressive development.

The development of socialist society is marked by steady progress. This is one of the principal distinctions in the way the law of negation of the negation operates under socialism.

The sources of its unprecedented progress are to be found in the very nature of the socialist system, in the great ideas of communism.

Of course a certain advance, which is fairly rapid when conditions are favourable, takes place in capitalist society too.

But there this movement is limited and one-sided. Priority development is given to those branches of industry which bring the employers big profits; this especially applies to plants working on military contracts. Under capitalism periods of advance give way to periods of deep recession, of crisis.

In socialist society, on the other hand, progress is continuous in all spheres of economic, political and cultural life. This is strikingly demonstrated by the high rates of development.

Industrial growth rates in the USSR are considerably higher than in the more industrialised capitalist countries. The Soviet Union needed 40 years to increase industrial output 30 times, while it took the United States, Britain and Germany from 80 to 150 years to make similar progress. Moreover, in these 40 years the USSR had to fight in devastating wars which wrought great destruction in the national economy and retarded its development.

Great changes have taken place in agriculture since the establishment of Soviet rule. Once a backward, petty-goods peasant economy, it is now a large-scale socialist economy capable of supplying industry with raw materials and the population with food products in ever increasing quantities.

Soviet science and culture have many achievements to their credit. Not so long ago the country was backward with nearly 80 per cent of the population illiterate, but it has now become a land of universal literacy where the transition to universal secondary education has been completed in the main. Soviet universities and colleges train millions of highly-qualified specialists. Artificial satellites of the Earth and Moon, powerful space rockets and interplanetary spaceships, atomic power plants, the first in history manned orbital space flights of Soviet citizens attest to the enormous scientific progress in the USSR.

It would be wrong, however, to assume that under socialism progress follows a straight line. Here too development has a spiral-like character and in various spheres of social life there is a certain repetition of stages already passed.

In particular this applies to economic management in the USSR, democracy, socialist emulation, culture, public education and other spheres where some of the current forms and methods are, so to say, a revival and development of the old but only on a new, deeper and broader foundation which makes for their fuller development and maximum efficiency.

Hence, this is not an absolute repetition, not a mechanical imitation of the old but a qualitatively new state, a transition to a higher level with the preservation of positive experience.

The first communist *subbotnik* that was organised in Soviet Russia in 1919, for example, signified a prompt accomplishment of the production tasks. It was shock work of the workers at their jobs: a group of workers at a Moscow marshalling yard repaired locomotives and carriages and performed loading and unloading operations in their off-work hours without remuneration, in the course of which their productivity of labour was higher than during the ordinary performance of their duties. This *subbotnik* attracted Lenin's attention and he called it a "great beginning".

Later, however, communist *subbotniks* were chiefly organised for the purpose of fulfilling various auxiliary tasks, including the cleaning of production premises and compounds, city blocks, construction sites, etc. This was a justified measure during the periods of economic dislocation and economic rehabilitation. But with the growth of socialist production such *subbotniks* led to the elimination of personal responsibility and irrational use of qualified manpower, which divested communist *subbotniks* of their basic principle, shock work in off-work hours at places of employment.

Recently, the original form of the *subbotniks* has been revived, but on an incomparably higher level. Today the entire Soviet people, the masses, and not merely individual groups of workers take part in them. The communist *subbotniks* which are organised on the anniversaries of Lenin's birth are nation-wide shock-work shifts of the people at their work places. The enormous economic and moral effect of these *subbotniks* leaves the old indicators far behind.

* * *

In this chapter we have discussed the basic laws of materialist dialectics. These laws furnish the key to understanding universal motion and development in the material world, reveal their sources and driving forces which are contained in internal contradictions. These laws disclose the leap-like, progressive character of development; they show that reality makes progress through constant replacement, through negation of the old by the new.

To gain a better idea of development we should now turn to the main categories of materialist dialectics.

CHAPTER VII

Categories of Materialist Dialectics

Any science, no matter what sphere of material reality it investigates, is not only a system of laws, but also of definite categories, i.e., the most general concepts which are elaborated in the process of development of each science and constitute its foundation. In mechanics, for example, such concepts are: mass, energy, force; in political economy—commodity, value, money, and so on.

In generalising the achievements of science and people's practical activity, philosophy has its own system of categories. *Philosophical categories* are concepts reflecting the general features and connections, sides and properties of reality. We have already analysed certain major categories in our study of philosophical materialism. These are first of all the categories of matter and consciousness, then motion, space and time. Studying the basic laws of Marxist dialectics, we have also examined such categories as contradiction, quantity, quality, leap, negation. In this chapter we shall discuss one more group of categories: the *particular* and the *universal, content* and *form, essence* and *phenomenon, cause* and *effect, necessity* and *chance, possibility* and *reality.*

A study of these categories will considerably broaden our understanding of the universal development and connections of the material world, the basic laws of Marxist dialectics.

The laws and categories of dialectics are interconnected. When we studied the basic laws of Marxist dialectics we learned that they, in effect, represent the relationship or connection of categories. The law of the passage of quantitative into qualitative changes, for example, expresses a definite connection of the categories of quantity and quality, etc. Hence, without a knowledge of categories it is impossible to comprehend the laws. On the other hand, knowledge of the laws enables us to understand the essence of categories of dialectics. The law of the unity and conflict of opposites thus makes it possible to reveal the real meaning of such antithetical categories as content and form, necessity and chance, possibility and reality, etc.

Before proceeding to discuss particular categories, let us ascertain their origin and consider some of their common features.

1. Origin and Common Features of the Categories of Dialectics

The categories of Marxist dialectics are *a result, a generalisation of the centuries-old experience of people, of their labour and knowledge*. In the course of his practical activity man, coming in contact with, and cognising objects and phenomena of the world, has singled out their essential, general features and has fixed the results in categories, concepts. Categories of cause and effect, content and form and others took shape in man's mind as he came into contact, billions of times, with objectively existing causes and effects, the content and form of definite material bodies and other major aspects of reality. Hence categories are a result of man's practical and cognitive activity, a stage in his knowledge of the world around him. "Man is confronted with a *web* of natural phenomena," Lenin wrote. "Instinctive man, the savage, does not distinguish himself from nature. Conscious man does distinguish: categories are stages of distinguishing, i.e., of cognising the world."*

A result of practice and knowledge, the categories of materialist dialectics are of great importance for man's practical and cognitive activities. As stepping stones to knowledge, they help people to find their way in the intricate web of phenomena in nature and society, reveal the interconnection and interdependence of things, the definite order and the law-governed character of their development, and to choose the right course of practical activity.

Marxist dialectics discloses the essence of categories, the sources of their origin and above all emphasises their *objective* character. Categories have their source in objects and phenomena existing independent of man and reflect their most general, essential features. Categories of cause and effect thus reflect the objectively existing relation between objects and processes, by which some of them cause other objects and processes to come into being, these latter being their effect.

In contrast to materialism, idealism denies the objective character of categories. From the point of view of subjective idealists, for example, categories exist only in the consciousness of man and have no relation to reality. The German philosopher Immanuel Kant maintained that before man begins to cognise the world his consciousness already contains categories of causality, necessity, chance, etc., which allegedly helps him to introduce order into the chaotic world of natural phenomena. Present-day subjective idealists, the neo-positivists in particular, also claim that categories are

* V.I. Lenin, "Conspectus of Hegel's Book *The Science of Logic*", *Collected Works*, Vol. 38, p. 93.

general concepts which are connected only with the direct sense-emotions of the subject and have no relation to the objective world existing independent of man. While paying lip service to the objective character of categories, the objective idealist Hegel in fact regarded them as stages, moments in the development of the absolute idea, the universal spirit.

Idealist views of the origin of categories are absolutely untenable. Practical activity, the development of science and people's personal experience show that categories were not invented by man, but discovered by him in objective reality.

From the standpoint of Marxist dialectics categories have other important features, namely *interconnection, changeability* and *mobility* which reflect the unity of the material world itself, the universal connection, interaction and development of its objects and phenomena. Categories are so closely connected that under certain conditions one can turn into another; thus, cause becomes effect and vice versa, necessity becomes chance and chance turns into necessity, and so on. Categories are not only interconnected, but also changeable and mobile. As they reflect the constatly developing material world, they themselves change.

Metaphysicians of all sorts misrepresent the dialectical nature of categories. As a rule, they separate categories from one another, ignoring the role played by some of them and absolutising the significance of others. And this perverts reality and often leads to reactionary political conclusions.

In order to comprehend the true nature of categories and use them as an instrument of scientific cognition and practical activity, they have to be approached from the standpoint of dialectical materialism. Later, when we examine separate categories, we shall endeavour to show their scientific and practical significance.

In studying the material world, man first of all notices the countless multitude of particular, individual objects and phenomena. Then, comparing them, he singles out features and connections that they have in common. We shall do the same and begin the examination of categories with the individual and the universal.

2. The Individual and the Universal

What Is the Individual and the Universal?

Every object possesses a number of particular, intrinsic features. Let us take the poplar next to our home. It has size, a certain number of branches arranged in a particular way, special configuration of the roots and some other features.

Every man has his own idiosyncrasies, abilities and habits, interests and inclinations, gait and manner of speech. This is what singles him out from hundreds of millions of other people inhabiting our planet.

The poplar, the man, the individual object or phenomenon of the material world are the *individual* or the *particular*.

Anything particular or individual, however, does not exist by itself; it is connected with other objects and phenomena. A man lives on Earth where there are many other people. He has much in common with them, being connected with them by thousands of the most diverse threads. He has a vocation, and this means that he possesses some features inherent in all people of that vocation. Man belongs to a definite class and a definite nation, therefore he has certain national and class distinctions. All people possess such features as anatomo-physiological structure, ability to feel and think, to work and speak, etc. Similarly, each object, besides having its own peculiar, individual features, has features in common with other objects.

The *universal* is that which is present in many individual, particular objects. While individual features set the given object apart from others, the universal draws it together with these other objects, connects it with them and places it in a definite species or class of homogeneous objects.

Dialectics of the Individual and the Universal

The individual and the universal are found in dialectical unity in any object. On the one hand, the individual contains the universal. It exists only in the connection that leads to the universal. Each individual organism is thus connected with the universal, the species to which it belongs and with which it has common features; and through the species it is connected with what is even more universal, the genus. Taking into account the connection of the particular with the universal, the existence of the universal in the particular, dialectical materialism considers that *each particular is universal in one way or another.*

On the other hand, the universal exists only in the particular or through the particular. There is not a single species of plant or animal outside individual plants or animals. Being universal in relation to the individual, the species does not embrace all the features of the individual organisms it includes, but only the essential, recurring ones. That is why Lenin described the universal as a *side* or *essence* of the particular.

The individual and the universal are not only interconnected but also change constantly. The boundary between them is not fixed. In certain conditions, during development, they pass into one another: the particular becomes the universal, and vice versa.

In the development of organisms there have been instances when a new, useful characteristic acquired by an *individual* organism is transmitted by heredity, and in time becomes common to the mass, the vast number of individual organisms, i.e., it turns into a *universal* characteristic, a distinctive of the species. If, however, a *universal* characteristic loses its significance for the vital processes of the species, it gradually withers away, becomes atrophied and in succeeding generations will only seldom occur; it may be met in *individual* organisms as an atavism, a reversion to the organisation of remote ancestors. Here the universal has turned into the individual.

Dialectics of the universal and the individual manifests itself in social phenomena as well.

Let us examine the rise and significance of communist *subbotniks* in the light of the principled assessment that was made by Lenin who perceived in a single, and what seemed to be an ordinary, fact a general law of the development of communist society.

The participation of the workers in the first *subbotnik* turned the latter into a great beginning because it inaugurated a mass movement for a communist attitude to labour which developed into a method of building a new society.

In the incredibly difficult conditions of the civil war, economic dislocation and famine the workers set the first examples of communist labour; they voluntarily participated in the *subbotnik* in their off-work hours without expecting to receive any benefits or honours, and their labour productivity on that day was the highest ever attained in those times.

In Lenin's opinion this was a turning point in the consolidation of the new system.

He regarded this as a revolution in the consciousness of the working people, a revolution in the attitude to the future of society, a revolution in the attitude to labour. Were it not for this revolution it would have been impossible to build a new society. He pointed out that it was up to the masses themselves to build living, creative socialism, that the strength and invincibility of the new social system lay in the consciousness of the people, in the fact that the masses, displaying unprecedented heroism and self-sacrifice, did this willingly, fully convinced that the new system was consistent with their fundamental, vital interests. That explains why the emergence and development of the sense of being master of his land is a distinguishing feature of the new man.

Lenin believed that communism really began when masses of workers and peasants started to show concern for rehabilitating and promoting production, for protecting the products which were made available to society as a whole, to all the working people.

Of course, a revolution in the consciousness of the working people, development of a communist attitude to work, did not take place instantaneously; it was a gradual process but one which developed and is continuing to develop in all fields of activity on the basis of a new system, embracing ever new sections of the working people and acquiring ever new forms.

Today there is every reason to say that these individual shoots of communism have turned into universal ones and have become part and parcel of the life of the new society in the USSR and in other socialist countries; they are also becoming universal in the socialist-oriented developing countries where their new forms are of international theoretical and practical interest.

The competition for the title of shock-workers and communist-labor collectives is the highest form of socialist emulation in the USSR. In Moscow, for instance, there are more than two million shock-workers of communist labour and about 200 communist-labour collectives (enterprises and organisations).

The working masses in the People's Democratic Republic of Yemen, demonstrating a highly conscious attitude to the solution of acute economic problems, voluntarily agreed to a temporary reduction in wages and an increase in the working day.

The citizens of Cotonou in the People's Republic of Benin cultivated thousands of acres of vacant land near their city in the course of "red Saturdays". As a result, factory and office collectives and the personnel of educational institutions now have their own plantations which contribute to a higher living standard of the working people. Thanks to these same "red Saturdays" in the course of which all people come out into the streets with brooms and spades, Cotonou is now one of the tidiest towns on the Western coast of Africa.

In order to speed up the solution of the housing problem in the Democratic Republic of Afghanistan the workers and employees of the

Kabul housebuilding factory voluntarily turned up for work on their day off thus accelerating the production of items needed by the people's state.

And so, the "great beginning" is turning into a universal initiative reflecting the growing role and diversity of forms of the history-making activity of the masses.

Importance of the Categories of the Individual and the Universal for Practical Activities

It is very important in scientific and practical activities to take into account the dialectics of the individual and the universal. Only knowledge of the interconnection, the dialectics of the individual and the universal enables us to find our way in the maze of diverse processes of objective reality, to discover the laws of its development and apply them properly in practice. Moreover, knowledge of the universal and its connection with the particular forms the basis of scientific forecasts, makes it possible not only to disclose important features of known objects and phenomena, determine their main course, the direction of their development, but also to deduce the existence of other particular objects and processes so far unknown to man. Mendeleyev, for example, proceeding from the periodic law of chemical elements which revealed their most general properties, deduced the existence of four chemical elements unknown at that time. Later he described in detail the properties of three of them. After a certain time these elements (gallium, scandium and germanium) were discovered.

Strict account of the interaction of the individual and the universal is of great importance in social life, especially at the present time when mankind is making the great transition from capitalism to communism. The course of this transition largely depends on the correct solution to the question of the correlation between the general laws of the socialist revolution and national distinctions in one country or another. That is why such an acute worldwide ideological struggle is now being fought on this issue.

It is clear from the experience of socialist construction in the USSR and other countries that the replacement of capitalism in all countries is a uniform revolutionary process which has *common, fundamentally important laws*. In the first place, they are the leading role of the Marxist-Leninist party—the party and vanguard of the working class; the consolidation of the power of the working class in one form or another; the transformation of the economy and all social relations along socialist lines; and defence of the revolution against all attacks by class enemies.

Present-day nationalists and revisionists ignore the general laws governing socialist development; they absolutise the individual, concrete national conditions of various countries. In contrast to the theory of scientific communism, they promote unscientific ideas of "national communism" which, in effect, is renunciation of the socialist revolution. These ideas are wholly repudiated by the entire course of the international working-class and communist movement.

Dogmatists, on the other hand, ignore the need to take into account concrete historical conditions in a revolution. They claim that revolutions every where are made according to one and the same pattern pre-cast once and for all. What makes this position harmful is that it belittles the creative initiative of the masses, undermines their faith in socialism and thereby greatly impedes the movement towards socialism.

Marxism-Leninism, while pointing out that these general laws are indispensable for the transition to socialism, does not at all ignore the national distinctions of each country. On the contrary, it calls for the creative application of these laws to concrete historical conditions. No two countries have the same level of economic development, nor the same correlation of class forces, nor the same historical and national traditions. All this taken together determines the specific features and distinctions in the forms and methods of building socialism and the pace of socialist changes in various countries. It is a key task of Marxist parties to take into account the national features of each individual country and to find the forms and methods of applying the general laws of socialist revolution in it.

Now that we have given an idea of the particular and shown that it is bound up with the universal, we shall go further into it and find out what are the particular objects, things and phenomena which man constantly encounters.

The category of content and form gives an idea of what a given object actually is.

3. Content and Form

What Is Content and Form?

Content is the sum-total of elements and processes constituting the given object or phenomenon. *Form* is the structure, the organisation of the content. It is not something external in relation to content, but is inherent in it.

Elementary particles, and processes associated with their movement, make up the content of the atom of a chemical element. Their arrangement in the atom constitutes its form. Metabolism, irritability, contractibility and other processes, and also the organs, tissues and cells in which these processes take place make up the content of the living organism. The form of the living organism is represented by the way vital processes transpire in it and by the structure of its organs and tissues.

Content and form are inherent in all social phenomena as well. Thus, the productive forces (in particular the instruments of production and the people who use them) represent the content of a historically determined mode of production. Relations of production (the relations of people in the process of production based on their relation to these instruments) constitute the form of a mode of production.

Dialectical materialism proceeds from the *unity* of content and form, their inseparability. Both form and content are inherent in the given object and therefore cannot be separated from one another. There is no content in general, but only formed content, i. e., content which has a definite form. Similarly there is no pure form without any content. Form always has content; it presupposes a definite content whose structure or organisation it represents.

Decisive Significance of Content and Active Role of Form

Having learned that each object represents a unity of content and form, let us now examine how content and form are interconnected, how they interact in the process of the development of objects.

Content is very active. By virtue of its intrinsic contradictions it constantly develops, moves. Then, with the change in the content, the form also changes. *Content determines form.*

Let us trace, for example, the development of social production. It always begins with the content—the productive forces. In an effort to produce as much material wealth as possible, people constantly improve the instruments of production and increase their own skill. This inevitably leads to a change in the form of social production—the relations of production.

In nature, too, content determines form. From biology we know that a change in the conditions of existence of a living organism is followed at first by a change in its functions (the intrinsic type of metabolism and other processes which make up the content of life), by the appearance of new protein substances, etc. Only then, on the basis of the change in content, does the form—the organisation or structure of the organism—change as well. If, for example, a plant is transferred from a humid to a dry climate, its metabolism changes. This change will proceed in such a way as to enable the plant to obtain more and lose less moisture in the new conditions. The structure of the organism will change correspondingly: its roots will penetrate deeper into the soil, drawing additional moisture; the leaves will become narrower so that less moisture will be evaporated.

Although form is the product of content, it does not remain passive in relation to it. It *actively* influences content, facilitates or retards its development. A new form, corresponding to the content, promotes the latter's development. An old form, not corresponding to the content, however, retards its development. If we take as an example social production again, we shall find that its form, relations of production, not only depends on the content, but itself plays an active part in its development. Progressive, socialist relations of production, for example, ensure exceptionally high growth rates of industrial and agricultural output and an advance of the entire socialist economy. But production relations of contemporary capitalism restrain, hamper the development of productive forces, and at times result in their stagnation and even destruction.

It follows, therefore, that the role and significance of form in development must not be underestimated. Yet the opponents of Marxism, the opportunists, in their efforts to prevent the establishment of a revolutionary party of the new type, denied the role played by the party's organisational forms, declaring that the form was passive, inert and had no influence at all on the content of the revolutionary struggle.

Lenin overturned the opportunists and disclosed the enormous significance of organisational forms in the party's entire activity. In his work *One Step Forward, Two Steps Back* he formulated the party's organisational principles which were translated into life by the party of the new type which he founded. The organisational form of the Communist party, which is based on the principle of democratic centralism, enabled it successfully to guide the revolutionary struggle of the proletariat and the building of socialism.

In analysing the interaction of form and content we should also bear in mind that, depending on the conditions, one and the same content can develop in *different forms*.

The international communist movement knows from experience that the dictatorship of the proletariat, which makes up the content of the transition period from capitalism to socialism, is possible in more than one form. In the USSR the dictatorship of the proletariat had the form of the Soviets of working People's Deputies and in other countries of the world socialist system the form of People's Democracy. It is possible that the future may produce new forms of the dictatorship of the proletariat.

The diversity of forms reinforces the content, makes it richer and more varied, enables it to develop in the most different conditions. That is why in revolutionary struggle and socialist construction it is so important to be able to choose the forms which best of all suit the concrete historical conditions.

Contradiction Between Form and Content

In order to get a better idea of the correlation of content and form, it is important to explain its *contradictory* nature. We have already said that form is more stable than content. That is why it lags behind content's development, becomes obsolete and comes into contradiction with it. The contradiction between the old form and the new content usually culminates in rejection of the old form and its replacement by a new one, as a result of which content acquires scope for further development.

Thus, as conditions change, an organism is compelled to assimilate new nutritive substances. In connection with this, the content of the organism, i. e., its intrinsic metabolism and all its vital activity, changes more or less rapidly. As for the form, the structure of the organism, it does not keep pace with the development of the content and comes into contradiction with it. This contradiction is resolved by a change in the structure of the organism that brings it into conformity with the changed content. As a result, existing organs are transformed or new ones arise. For example, when organisms pass from an aquatic environment to conditions of amphibian life, they gradually develop lungs instead of gills, limbs instead of fins, etc.

In social life, too, there is contradiction between content and form, as is clearly demonstrated by the above example relating to the development of social production.

In the course of development the new content (productive forces) comes into contradiction with the old form (relations of production). This contradiction is resolved through the replacement of the obsolete relations of production by new ones which ensure the further unhindered development of the productive forces. Under capitalism the contradiction between the content and form of production is antagonistic. Hence the need for a socialist revolution whose mission is to replace the old, capitalist form of production with the new, socialist form.

Under socialism, too, for example in the USSR, there its a contradiction between the form and the content of social production. But this contradiction is not of an antagonistic character and is successfully eliminated by the Soviet people led by the Communist Party.

By overcoming these and other contradictions and difficulties, Soviet people dispense with the old, obsolete forms hindering socialist construction. At the same time the process of improving all forms of economic, political and cultural life of Soviet society steadily continues.

Now that we have examined what the content and form of an object are, let us see whether all its elements and aspects are equally important, whether all of them play an equal part in the existence and development of the given object. To answer this question we must examine the categories of essence and phenomenon.

4. Essence and Phenomenon

What Is Essence and Phenomenon?

The concept of essence is similar to the concept of content but is not identical with it. Whereas content represents the sum-total of *all* elements and processes constituting a given object, *essence* is the *chief, internal,* relatively stable side of an object (or the total of its sides and relations). Essence determines the nature of an object, all its other sides and characteristics follow from it.

Metabolism is the essence of a living organism. It underlies all the vital functions and comprises the inner nature of all living bodies. As Engels pointed out, from metabolism, which represents the essential function of protein, follow all other factors of life: irritability, contractibility, the possibility of growth, internal movement.*

In social phenomena essence also expresses the internal, chief side of processes. Describing imperialism, the higher stage of capitalism, Lenin defined it as monopoly capitalism. It is monopoly rule, which has replaced rivalry, that is the essence of imperialism. From the domination of the monopolies stem all other features of imperialism, above all the extraction of monopoly superprofits by those capitalists who are members of monopoly associations. In their quest for superprofits the imperialists form international monopoly unions and divide the world into their spheres of influence, monopolise finance, export capital instead of goods, and intensify the exploitation of the working people in their own countries and also of the peoples in the colonies and dependencies. All this extremely aggravates capitalism's intrinsic contradictions. Imperialism is the stage of decaying, moribund capitalism; it is the eve of the socialist revolution.

* See Frederick Engels, *Anti-Dühring*, pp. 104-05.

National liberation revolutions, too, have their essence, namely, to win national independence, cast off the political and economic oppression of world capitalism, promote national economies and culture, and create people's democratic states.

The essence of socialist society is the dominance of socialist property, absence of exploitation, planned economy, cooperation and mutual assistance of members of society, and the fullest satisfaction of the material and cultural requirements of the members of society through the development and improvement of production on the basis of advanced techniques.

What is a phenomenon? A *phenomenon is the outward, direct expression of essence, the form in which it is manifested.* Metabolism as the essence of everything living is revealed in the most diverse phenomena. It is manifested in the nearly half a million species of plants and about one and a half million species of animals. All of them differ from each other in appearance and degree of development; they assimilate nutrition, grow and propagate differently.

The essence of imperialism is manifested in the aggressive wars (world and local) which it unleashes; in the arms race; in the ever deepening general crisis (economic, political and moral) of capitalism; in the intensified exploitation of the labouring people; in the growing unemployment; in the decline in living standards; in the growth of crime; in the increasing exploitation of undeveloped and dependent countries, etc.

The essence of socialism is expressed in the following phenomena of daily Soviet life: the peaceful foreign policy of the USSR; the steady improvement of the Soviet people's wellbeing; large-scale construction of new factories and powerful electric stations; vigorous technical progress in the most diverse branches of the economy; the unprecedented pace of building houses and cultural establishments; reduction of the working day; rising wages; improvement of social maintenance and everyday services, etc.

Dialectics of Essence and Phenomenon

Having discussed what essence and phenomenon are, let us see in what relation they stand to each other.

By generalising scientific achievements and practice, dialectical materialism asserts the *unity* of essence and phenomenon which are interconnected and inseparable. Essence *appears phenomenally*, phenomenon is *essential*, Lenin wrote. Phenomenon is the selfsame essence as manifested in reality. The outward, surface side of reality, the individual properties, moments and sides of things make up the phenomenon. Essence is the same phenomena, the same multifarious moments, sides, but taken in their most stable, profound and general form. Lenin compared essence to a relatively calm, powerful and deep current of a swiftly flowing river, which on the surface has waves and foam. "...The foam above and the deep currents below. *But even the foam* is an expression of essence."*

Essence is necessarily revealed in each phenomenon, but not fully, only a certain small part of it. Phenomenon does not exhaust essence, but presents it from *one* side only.

There is no "pure" essence, i.e., the kind that would not manifest itself in anything. Every essence reveals itself in a mass of phenomena. The essence of socialism manifests itself through many events and facts of the socialist way of life.

Essence and phenomenon are not only indivisible, they are also *antithetical* and never fully coincide. Their antithesis is an expression of the internal contradictoriness of the objects of reality themselves. Essence is not seen on the surface, it is hidden and cannot be directly observed. It can be disclosed only in the course of prolonged comprehensive study of an object. If the form of manifestation and the essence of things coincided directly, Marx wrote, every science would be superfluous. It is the task of science to reveal essence, the internal, deep and underlying processes behind the multitude of phenomena, outward sides and features of reality.

Importance of the Categories of Essence and Phenomenon

Knowledge of the dialectics of essence and phenomenon is very important in social life, in science and practical activity.

This knowledge gives scientists the confidence that however complex the process of cognising the phenomena they study, however deeply essence is hidden behind these phenomena, it will eventually become known. Astronomers, for example, conducted thorough observations of the Sun for many years. With the aid of instruments they discovered spots and protuberances on the Sun and traced the fluxes of various particles emitted by the Sun. But all these phenomena by themselves gave no clue to the processes taking place within the Sun, to the source of solar energy. It took science a long time to discover the essence of the processes behind these phenomena. It was ascertained that a thermonuclear reaction (formation of helium from hydrogen) takes place in the Sun. It is the colossal energy

---

* V.I. Lenin, "Conspectus of Hegel's Book *The Science of Logic*", *Collected Works*, Vol. 38, p. 130.

released as a result of this reaction that maintains the very high temperature of the Sun.

Knowledge of essence is particularly indispensable because phenomena often tend to give a false idea of the character of processes. It seems to us, for example, that the Sun moves around the Earth, while in reality we know that the Earth moves around the Sun. It might seem that broad democracy exists in the imperialist world; after all, universal suffrage, freedom of speech, of the press, freedom to form political parties and groups, etc., are proclaimed there. But in reality democracy under imperialism is a mere deception, it is limited democracy, democracy only for the rich.

Knowledge based only on manifestations of essence, cannot give a correct picture of the world or serve as a guide to action. Inability to differentiate phenomenon from essence leads to serious mistakes in theory and practice.

The founders of Marxism-Leninism made unique analyses of the essence of social phenomena. Among them is the discovery by Marx of the essence of capitalist production which constituted a whole epoch in the development of social thought.

Bourgeois economists and sociologists, confining themselves to a study of phenomena, of what only appears to be true, have claimed, and continue to claim, that there is no exploitation in capitalist society, that the worker receives all that he earns from the capitalist. From their point of view, the source of capitalist profit is not the exploitation of the workers, but the capital invested by the capitalists in production.

What is the real state of affairs?

In reality the situation is entirely different. The worker needs a certain amount of means of subsistence for himself and for his family. To obtain them he is compelled to sell his labour to the capitalist. It may appear that an ordinary purchase-and-sale transaction takes place between the worker and the capitalist: the worker sells his labour and the capitalist buys it; the worker works, while the capitalist pays him wages.

Outwardly it seems to be an equal transaction between the capitalist and the worker. Bourgeois ideologists, limiting themselves to it, arrive at the absolutely false conclusion that under capitalism there is no exploitation. They do not want to see the true essence of capitalist production.

Marx did not confine himself to an analysis of the superficial phenomena of capitalist society. Behind the phenomenon, the semblance of an equal transaction between the capitalist and the worker, he disclosed the exploitative essence of capitalist production. Marx showed that labour power is a special commodity capable of producing material values. Moreover, the values it produces are worth much more than the wages paid by the capitalist. The capitalist pays for only part of the value of the goods produced by the worker and keeps the rest. It is this, and this only, that is the source of capitalist profit.

Marx's discovery of the essence of capitalist exploitation is of tremendous historical importance. It made it possible to reveal the basis of the antagonism between the bourgeoisie and the proletariat, to show why struggle between them is inevitable and ultimately leads to the socialist revolution and the fall of capitalism.

This classical example of how social phenomena should be analysed clearly shows the immense importance which knowledge of the essence of objects and processes has for science and revolutionary practice.

And so, we have analysed the individual and the universal, content and form, essence and phenomenon, i.e., everything that helps us to understand a given object or phenomenon. Objects and phenomena, however, do not exist in isolation, but are interconnected and none of them can be understood outside of this connection. To study an object in connection with others means above all to establish the cause of its origin. Now we shall examine the categories of cause and effect.

5. Cause and Effect

What Is Cause and Effect?

In the objective world we observe the constant interaction of phenomena, as a result of which some phenomena gave rise to others; these in turn give rise to still others, and so on. Friction, for example, causes heat, drought leads to crop failure, etc. The interaction of phenomena is also observed in social life. The national liberation movement, for example, has brought about the break-up of imperialism's colonial system.

A phenomenon or group of interacting phenomena which precede and give rise to another phenomenon or group are called *cause*. The phenomenon produced by the action of the cause is called *effect*.

Cause always *precedes* effect, but succession in time is not an adequate sign of cause. Day, for example, follows night, but night is not the cause of day. The alternation of day and night is caused by the rotation of the Earth on its axis. Causal dependence between two phenomena exists when one of them not only precedes the other, but inevitably *gives rise* to it.

Cause should not be confused with occasion. *Occasion* is an event which directly precedes the effect; it is not the cause itself, but sets it in motion. Thus, the legitimate assistance provided by the Soviet Union and Cuba to their natural allies—the peoples of Angola and Ethiopia—at the request of their governments for the purpose of repelling external aggression, was an occasion for a sharp intensification of aggressive actions by NATO countries on the African continent. Under the pretext of "saving" it from the "Soviet-Cuban threat" imperialism launched a crusade against independent Africa.

The true cause of this campaign is imperialism's desire to stop and reverse the mounting movement for national and social liberation on the African continent, re-establish full control over the immensely rich sources of mineral raw materials and fantastically cheap labour power, exploit them unscrupulously and obtain net superprofits.

Cause should also be distinguished from the *conditions* in which it operates. Productive labour is the cause of all social wealth. But for labour to produce wealth, an object of labour and tools for working on this object are needed. Neither the object of labour nor the tools bring wealth by themselves, but they are a necessary condition for man's labour.

Criticism of Anti-Marxist Views of Causality

In the material world causality has a general, universal character. No phenomena exist or can exist without cause, for everything has its cause. "There is no smoke without fire," as the old saying goes. Causality is objective, it has not been introduced into reality by man's reason or by some supernatural force. Causality is inherent in reality and is discovered by man in the process of cognition and practical activity.

The dialectical-materialist understanding of causality diametrically differs from the religious interpretation of the world, according to which God is the cause of everything existing: God supposedly created the world order and he refashions it, and divine will is the prime cause of everything existing. Religion also preaches the *teleological* theory of the world, which regards the development of the world as the realisation of some kind of supernatural, preordained aims. From the standpoint of teleology, Engels wrote, cats were created to eat mice, mice, to be eaten by cats, and all of nature to prove the wisdom of God.

There are, however, no preordained aims. Everything develops on the basis of natural causes, objective laws. It goes without saying that nature cannot and does not set itself any aims. In society the situation is different, because people act consciously, set themselves definite aims, and work to achieve them. These aims, however, are not preordained by the Almighty, but are determined by objective causes, by the entire course of historical development.

The doctrine that the natural course of things is subordinated to objective causality, governed by laws, is called *determinism.* Determinism is the opposite of *indeterminism,* an idealistic doctrine denying objective causality, necessity, laws. Indeterminism is an idealist approach to causality; it looks for the order, the causes of development of phenomena, not in the outside objective world, but in consciousness, in reason.

Dialectical materialism is opposed not only to indeterminism, but also to *mechanistic determinism,* which reduces the whole diversity of causes to outward, mechanical influences. Such determinism prevailed in natural science in the 17th and 18th centuries when mechanics was the most developed of all the natural sciences.

Mechanistic determinism may be applied in studying the movement of macro-bodies, in technical calculations of machines, bridges and other installations. But attempts to explain numerous biological processes, mental activity and social life from the point of view of mechanistic determinism are erroneous.

Mechanistic determinism also proved inapplicable to quantum mechanics, a new field of physics. The micro-particles studied by quantum mechanics qualitatively differ from the macro-bodies studied by classical mechanics. Whereas the co-ordinate (position in space) and speed of a macro-body can be determined exactly and simultaneously by the laws of classical mechanics, this cannot be done with an elementary particle. In the micro-world where the laws of classical mechanics are invalid, the laws of quantum mechanics operate. They make it possible to determine either the co-ordinate or the speed of the particle in each given moment of time, not with absolute accuracy, but only approximately, with a certain degree of probability.

When the opponents of materialism realised that mechanistic determinism cannot be applied to micro-objects they proclaimed the "collapse" of determinism in general and the triumph of indeterminism. They declared that causality in micro-processes is created by man himself in the course of observation and measuring operations. In reality, however, modern physics in no way refuted the dialectical-materialist principle of causality; on the contrary, it furnished additional proof of it. At the same time it showed that determinism appears in different ways in various spheres of reality.

Dialectical materialism is also opposed to the metaphysical separation of cause and effect. Proceeding from the achievements of science and practice, dialectical materialism asserts that cause and effect are *inseparably connected,* that there is no effect without cause and vice versa. The connection between cause and effect is of an internal, law-governed character.

This is the kind of connection in which effect stems from cause, is a result of its action. Engendered by cause, effect does not remain indifferent to its cause and exerts a reverse action upon it. Thus, economic relations between people in the process of production are *the* cause, the source of political, philosophical and other ideas, but these ideas, in turn, influence the development of economic relations.

The interconnection of cause and effect also means that one and the same phenomenon can be the cause in one connection and the effect in another. The combustion of coal in boilers at electric power plants is the cause of the conversion of water into steam. Steam, being the effect of coal combustion, is itself the cause of motion of the generator's rotor. Its rotation generates electricity, which is the source, the cause of motion of numerous machines and mechanisms giving people heat, light, etc. This train of argument could be taken further. What is characteristic of causality is this endless chain of reciprocal connections, the *universal interaction* of objects and phenomena of the world where each link is simultaneously both a cause and an effect.

Scientific and Practical Importance of Causality

Knowledge of the causal dependence of phenomena is extremely important in science and practice. By discovering the causes of useful phenomena man can facilitate their action and thereby accelarate the development of the useful phenomena and processes he needs. Knowing, for example, that good tillage, on-schedule sowing, irrigation, introduction of fertiliser, and other farming methods are the cause of high yields, we can considerably raise crop yields by constantly improving these methods.

Knowledge of the causes of harmful phenomena enables man to eliminate these phenomena, restrict their action and thereby prevent the onset of undesirable effects.

The ability to reveal the main causes of the given phenomenon is particularly important for practical activity. By discovering the main causes, people can understand the origin and essence of a phenomenon, its place in relation to other phenomena, and the laws governing its development.

The *main* cause is the one without which the given phenomenon could not arise; it determines the main features of this phenomenon.

What, for example, was the main cause of the Soviet people's victory over the Nazi invaders in the Second World War? This cause was the social and state system of the Soviet Union, the might of the Soviet Armed Forces, and not the vast territory or the rigorous Russian winter and similar claims put forward by bourgeois ideologists. The latter factors, although playing some part, were by no means the chief, determining causes.

The Communist Party always looks for the chief, decisive causes. The ability to pick them out from the innumerable other causes makes it possible to find that particular, *main link* in the chain of events, which enables the party and the people to cope with every task confronting them in any given period. Lenin maintained that the art of politics consists in finding this main link in the chain of social phenomena, grasping it firmly and thereby ensuring full success.

The CPSU believes that the main, decisive foreign policy link which can ensure the best conditions for the growth and the successes of the world forces of peace, democracy, national liberation and socialism, and the progress of the whole of mankind, is the Leninist policy of peaceful coexistence of states with different socio-political systems, international detente, universal and complete disarmament, a policy of mutually beneficial equal economic and cultural cooperation. This policy fully reflects the aspirations and vital interests of the peoples of the whole world and opens favourable prospects for the developing countries to solve their problems in conditions of peace. The foreign policy of the CPSU is designed to achieve the implementation of the Leninist principles of peaceful coexistence. Only by grasping this main and decisive link will the world's peace-loving forces be able to solve all vital problems confronting mankind.

Causality is the most general, universal connection. But it does not exhaust all the many connections of reality and represents, as Lenin pointed out, only a small part of the world connections. Necessary and chance connections are also very important in the intricate web of the world's causal connections. We shall now examine them.

6. Necessity and Chance

What Is Necessity and Chance?

In order to understand necessity and chance let us first answer the following question: are all the events necessary in given conditions? Must all of them proceed in a certain way and not in any other way?

We know that if a seed is planted it will germinate, given moisture and heat. But the young plant may perish as a result of a downpour. Are both these events (the germination of the seed and the perishing of the plant) necessary?

Not both of them. Our day-to-day experience tells us that the germination of the seed in given conditions, i.e., in the presence of corresponding heat and moisture, is necessary. Such is the nature of the plant itself. But the downpour is something which might or might not have been, and it might have destroyed or merely damaged the plant. The downpour does not at all follow from the nature of the plant and was not necessary in the given conditions.

A phenomenon or event which, under definite conditions, must take place is called *necessity* (in our example the germination of the seed is a necessity). Day follows night, one year follows another necessarily. The birth and growth of the communist movement of the working class under capitalism is a necessity. It is engendered by the living conditions of the working class, its social position and its historical tasks.

Necessity follows from the essence, the internal nature of the developing phenomenon. It is constant and stable for the given phenomenon.

In contrast to necessity, *chance* (in our example the destruction of the plant by the downpour) need not necessarily happen. In the given conditions it might occur and it might not occur, it might proceed in one way or in another. Chance does not follow from the nature of the given object, it is unstable and temporary. But chance is not without cause. Its cause is not in the object itself, but outside of it—in external conditions.

Dialectics of Necessity and Chance

Necessity and chance are dialectically interconnected. One and same event is necessary and accidental simultaneously—necessary in one respect and accidental in another. The same downpour, being accidental in regard to the destruction of the plant, is a necessary effect of the atmospheric conditions in the area where it happened.

In contrast to dialecticians, metaphysicians deny the interconnection of necessity and chance. Some of them recognise only necessity and deny the possibility of chance factors in development. From their point of view, everything is inevitable, necessary, and therefore man is powerless to do anything about it, and must passively await the inevitable, inexorable course of events. Other philosophers recognise only chance, which in effect means renunciation of science, and refusal to recognise man's ability to foresee the course of events and to direct them.

Necessity and chance can pass into one another: what is chance in certain conditions is necessity in other, different conditions, and vice versa. In primitive society, for example, the exchange of commodities had an accidental character. Everything produced by a commune was as a rule consumed by it. With the rise and development of private property the exchange of goods was extended, and under capitalism it turned into objective necessity.

Necessity and chance do not exist in isolation from each other. In a process necessity appears as the main direction, the trend of development, but this trend breaks its way through a mass of chance phenomena. Chance *supplements* necessity, is *a form of its manifestation*. The mass of chance phenomena always conceals objective necessity or law. Chance serves as the form for the manifestation of necessity in social development too.

Importance of the Categories of Necessity and Chance

In science and practice it is very important to take into account the objective dialectics of necessity and chance. The task of science is to discover the internal, necessary connections behind the external appearances, the numerous chance events and connections. Knowledge of the laws, of objective necessity enables man to subordinate the numerous phenomena of nature and social life to his needs. Every science must primarily aim at cognition of necessity. The task of social science is, therefore, to reveal the objective necessity of social development and, on the basis of this cognised necessity, to transform the social order in the interests of the workers.

Science, however, should not ignore chance. Since accidents occur and exert some kind of influence on life, science must take into account their role in development, and protect man from them.

In different historical conditions the interconnection of necessity and chance is not identical. The dominance of capitalist property determines the spontaneous operation of necessity in capitalist conditions. The law of value, the law of anarchy and competition break their way through a mass of chance events and this means that under capitalism people are deprived of the opportunity to plan the life of society. They are mere toys of these spontaneous forces. Market is the necessary regulator of capitalist production, but it operates through numerous accidental fluctuations of market prices, which depend on similarly accidental changes in supply and demand. The distribution of labour under capitalism is also accidental. All this creates insecurity for the worker—he may become unemployed and lose his means of livelihood at any moment. Even the businessman has no peace of mind under capitalism, particularly the small or medium employer who may be ruined at any moment, because he cannot withstand the competition of more powerful rivals.

It should be noted, however, that state-monopoly regulation and prognostication of economic development are becoming widespread in capitalist countries. But quite often this sort of regulation does not transcend monopoly limits. Moreover, it does not eliminate market fluctuations which continue to be the main regulator of capitalist production in general.

The chaos on the capitalist market most seriously affects the peasants, farmers and agricultural workers, particularly in the developing countries where it puts them on the verge of physical extinction and dooms to chronic undernourishment, inevitable ruin and impoverishment. Moreover, in view of the specifics of agricultural production resulting directly from natural causes, the chance events occurring in nature have the most devastating effects in these countries. It is not by accident that drought, floods, hurricanes and other calamities of nature result in national tragedy, the loss of millions of human lives, millions of head of cattle, etc.

Socialism alone puts an end to the devastating play of chance. It ensures the planned, steady growth of agricultural production and of the living standards of all people engaged in it.

The promotion of this growth is a national task, and involves the efforts of other branches of the economy and many sciences.

Such an approach to agriculture in the USSR has made it possible to place its resources at the service of the people and to carry out such immense transformations as the development of enormous tracts of virgin and fallow lands, irrigate 16 million hectares of land and drain 15.2 million hectares.

Relying on their own social advantages and the assistance of the CMEA member states, some socialist-oriented developing countries have also started work on gigantic projects of subduing the elements. For instance, the planting of a green belt has been going on in Algeria since 1973. This green belt, a forest strip 1,500 kilometres long and 20 kilometres wide, will hold back the advancing sands of the Sahara which annually consume approximately 200,000 hectares of land.

Under socialism, due to the operation of its inherent laws, people have an opportunity to foresee the course of history and plan their activities accordingly in all spheres of life. Social necessity appears in the conscious, purposive activity of people. National economic plans in the USSR are witnesses to the skilful use of the objective necessity of social development.

The effect of chance in socialist society is greatly reduced by the conscious, planned effort of the people led by the Communist Party. Accidents occur, however, even under socialism. Sometimes due to chance circumstances some branches of industry or agriculture lag behind, individual factories do not fulfil their plans, etc. This leads to some disproportions and discrepancies in the development of the economy.

Accidents are also caused by weather conditions, drought, floods, storms, etc.

The Communist Party and the Soviet Government strive to reduce to a minimum the adverse influence of chance in society. To these ends improvements are constantly being made in the planning and organisation of production, and the latest scientific achievements are applied. A ramified system of state reserves is built up to meet exigencies.

Necessity always appears in definite objective conditions. But these conditions change, and so necessity, too, changes and develops. Each new necessity, however, does not arise in a ready, fully-shaped form, but at first exists merely as a possibility and turns into reality only in given favourable conditions.

Let us examine the categories of possibility and reality.

7. Possibility and Reality

What Is Possibility and Reality?

The new, the developing is necessary, but it does not arise at once. At first only definite prerequisites, factors making for its birth appear; these prerequisites then mature, develop, and by virtue of the operation of objective laws, the new object or phenomenon arises. These prerequisites for the birth of the new, which are present in the existing, are called *possibilities*. Thus, every germ possesses the possibility of development, of transformation into an adult organism. The adult organism which develops from the germ is a reality. *Reality* is the achieved, realised possibility.

Possibilities stem from objective laws, are engendered by them. The law of the unity of the organism and the environment, for example, creates the possibility, through a change of external conditions, to act purposively on organisms, to create new species of plants and animals. Here, needless to say, it is necessary to take account of the heredity of the organism which in the final analysis determines the direction of its change. The law of planned, proportionate development of the national economy under socialism creates the possibility of planning, etc.

Since objects and phenomena of the world are contradictory, possibilities, too, are contradictory. We should differentiate between *progressive* (positive) and *reactionary* (negative) possibilities. Any social revolution, for example, contains both the positive possibility of victory by the progressive forces and the negative possibility of victory by the reactionary forces. But, owing to the operation of history's objective laws, the progressive possibilities ultimately triumph, while victory of reactionary possibilities, although it occurs in some instances, is only temporary, transitory. The victory of reaction in the Russian revolution of 1905-07, for example, was temporary. A few years later, in 1917, the working class, in alliance with the peasants, won a decisive victory, first over tsarism, and then over the bourgeoisie.

Like everything in the world, possibilities are in *constant motion:* some of them grow, while others diminish. The USSR was the first nation to break the chain of imperialism and for several years was surrounded by imperialist states. That is why immediately after the victory of the Revolution, alongside the possibility of socialism's victory there was a certain possibility of the restoration of capitalism. As the strength of the Soviet Union grew, the possibility of socialism's complete victory steadily increased and became reality. *"Socialism,"* it is stressed in the programme of the CPSU, *"which Marx and Engels scientifically predicted as inevitable and the plan for the construction of which was mapped out by Lenin, has become a reality in the Soviet Union."** On the other hand, as socialism advanced, the possibilities of restoring capitalism steadily diminished and now practically no longer exist, because there are no forces in the world which could restore capitalism in the Soviet Union and crush the mighty socialist community. The victory of socialism in the USSR is complete and final.

Marxist dialectics differentiates between abstract and real possibilities.

An *abstract* (formal) possibility is one which cannot be realised in the given historical conditions. The possibility of a collision between planets of the solar system and other large celestial bodies, for example, is abstract: the chance of its occurrence is infinitesimally small.

Abstract, formal possibility must not be confused with the impossible. The impossible can never be realised because it runs counter to objective laws. It is impossible, for example, to reconcile the interests of the bourgeoisie and the working class. Abstract possibility does not run counter to objective laws and, in principle, can become reality, but only when the appropriate conditions mature.

A *real* possibility has prerequisites for realisation in given definite historical conditions. For example, the possibility of liberating all the colonies and dependent countries from foreign dependence is real. This process is in fact taking place at present.

---

* *Road to Communism*, Moscow, 1962, p. 459.

The distinctions between abstract and real possibilities are relative. In the process of development an abstract possibility can become real. Only a few years ago the possibility of man's flight to other planets was abstract because the technical facilities were lacking. Now, this possibility has become real, particularly after the world's first orbital flights of Soviet cosmonauts. Man has already set foot on the Moon and the time is not far off when he will set foot on other planets of the solar system. The dream of Utopian Socialists early in the 19th century about the possibility of transition to socialism was abstract: at that time the force necessary for socialism had not yet matured, there was no adequately organised revolutionary proletariat. But in the present epoch this possibility has become real and has already turned into reality in a large part of the world.

Conversion of Possibility into Reality Under Socialism

In nature, possibility turns into reality spontaneously, unconsciously. In society, on the other hand, the purposive, conscious activity of people is of decisive importance in the realisation of possibilities. Without the intervention of man, acting on the basis of cognised laws, possibility does not turn into reality. The possibility of preserving peace which exists at present is becoming reality as a result of the vigorous efforts of all the peace-loving forces.

No task is more important today than that of uniting all people of good will for the struggle in defence of peace. The number of peace supporters and their prestige are growing on all the continents; the various trends and organisations working for peace are displaying greater unity and coordination. The movement for peace is becoming more and more massive and international in character, and public opinion is playing an increasing role in the fight against those who sermonise the fatal inevitability of war and against the arms race, in dispelling the myth about a "Soviet threat" and unmasking the aggressive maneuvres of imperialism and neocolonialism.

In the course of their practical activities, transforming the world, people discover the intrinsic possibilities and work to turn them into reality. In socialist conditions it is particularly important to take into account real possibilities and work for their realisation.

The Soviet socialist system contains immense possibilities for economic, political and cultural progress. These possibilities are ably taken into account and realised in good time by the Communist Party of the Soviet Union which carefully supports and nurtures the shoots of the new, the progressive. Everyone in socialist society is interested in the realisation of progressive possibilities and that is why they are being rapidly turned into reality.

The possibility of building socialism, which arose as a result of the October Socialist Revolution, was realised by the Soviet people in a very brief period. The building of socialism gave rise to another possibility that is of the utmost importance for humanity—the real possibility of building communism.

The Soviet Union now has a social system of tremendous creative force; a powerful industry equipped with first-class machinery, a large-scale mechanised agriculture; advanced science; highly-qualified personnel capable of accomplishing the most complex tasks; domination of the all-conquering Marxist-Leninist teaching; and leadership by the wise, battle-tested Party. The country's natural wealth is vast and this is a prerequisite for unlimited economic development.

8. A System: Its Components, Structure, Functions, History and Environment

The dialectical principles of unity and diversity among the connections and interactions found in the movement and development of objects and phenomena are specifically expressed in a group of categories that relate to the *systems* understanding of reality. Let us consider these categories.

The Integral System

Take a molecule of water. It is formed of atoms of hydrogen and oxygen, but its properties differ from the properties of both its components. Hydrogen burns, oxygen is required for burning and water is used to put out fire.

Characterising cooperation as the totality of interacting producers, Marx observed that the "sum total of the mechanical forces exerted by isolated workmen differs from the social force that is developed when many hands take part simultaneously in one and the same undivided operation. . ."* In cooperation (which is also a system), a new productive force is created, a force that is essentially a mass phenomenon. Social contact itself, the interaction between different workers, gives rise to an "emulation and a stimula-

---

* *Capital I*: p. 308.

tion of the animal spirits that heighten the efficiency of each individual workman."*

An *integral system* thus functions as a totality of objects whose reciprocal action *gives rise to new integrated properties that are not possessed by the individual components of the system.*

There are *material* systems (atoms, molecules, organisms, socioeconomic formations, etc., which exist objectively) and *ideal* systems (science as a totality of logical forms).

Marx frequently attacked the "German-professor method" of linking concepts irrespective of objective reality. Lenin insisted on studying society as a social organism, a "definite system of production relations... a definite social formation."** A socioeconomic formation is the most universal form of social integrity, the basic form of the existence of social matter.

Components of a System

Each integral system is made up of a set of *components*. An atom, for instance, consists of a nucleus and electrons. A living organism, whether plant or animal, is formed of cells, tissue and organs. In the case of society, the situation is more complex. The material components of a social system are the means of production and the objects of consumption. Then there are non-material components like ideas, principles, norms and rules of social conduct. Economic, sociopolitical and cultural *processes* are characteristic of society.

The material and the non-material components as well as processes cannot exist without human beings. They produce the means of production and make use of the objects of consumption. People form the ideas and create the cultural values by which they are governed in labour and in life. Thus, man as a social entity functions as the universal component of a social system.

The Structure of a System

Enormous importance in defining the qualitative specifics of a system and its characteristics and properties is attached to its *structure*. It is the *method of interconnection and interaction of its components.*

The specifics of the structure depend primarily on the nature of the system's components. The interaction and connections between the ele-

---

* *Ibid.*, p. 309.
** Lenin, *Collected Works*, 1: p. 189.

mentary particles in an atom are one thing, the connections between the organs and tissues of a living organism another. Quite another still is the interaction and relations among people, things, processes and ideas that occur in society. Even so, though structure depends on the nature of the components, it plays an important role in a system. It links components together, transforms them and gives them a kind of integrality. Primarily, it determines the type of new properties that appear and that are not present in any of the individual components. The specific nature of interactions of atoms making up a molecule results in a new property which the individual atoms themselves do not have.

Of particular importance for the durability of a system is the *relative independence and stability of its structure*. Changes in the components of a system to not immediately, directly or automatically affect the structure. Within certain boundaries it remains permanent, thereby retaining the system as a whole. Thus, within a given socioeconomic formation the change of components takes place permanently. Technology is replaced by newer and better technology; one generation of people is replaced by another. But the basic structure of the system, the internal connections between its components and particularly the relations of *production* remain the same. Only a social revolution which establishes new relations of production radically changes the properties of the social system. One formation gives place to another which is more progressive. A structure is that which conditions the accumulation of quantitative changes within a system that are a necessary prerequisite for its subsequent development and transformation.

The Functions of a System

A system, particularly in society, is active and this appears in the *functions of its components*. Functions, according to Marx, "are but so many modes of giving free scope to [the individual's] own natural and acquired powers."* A living organism fulfills various functions, the most important of which are metabolism and reproduction. The organs and tissues of the living organism have their own specific functions—blood circulation, breathing, digestion, etc. The functions of the components, and this is important to note, help support the life of the organism as a whole.

A social system also fulfills its functions. The most important of these under capitalism is the production and accumulation of surplus value,

---

* *Capital, I*: p. 458.

profit. Socialism has a totally different function—to provide the ever-increasing satisfaction of the material and cultural needs of all members of society.

It is important to note that functions are "attached" to components and carried out within the framework of a system's structure, its internal organisation. Therefore, changes in the nature of components, in the character of their interaction (i.e.,in their structure) necessarily give rise to corresponding changes in the functions both of the components themselves and of the system as a whole.

Systems Factors

The *systems factors* are those forces, mechanisms and organs which together with the structure of a system ensure the maintenance of its qualitative specifics as well as its functioning and development.

The most common, universal systems factor is the *material unity of the world*, the dialectical principle of the interaction among objects and phenomena, which acquires a unique specific form in each particular type of system. Thus in biological and social systems it takes the form of *control*. In the higher animals the organ of control is the nervous system. In society there are two types of control, which have developed and still exist—the spontaneous and the conscious. The capitalist economy and society as a whole are controlled by the *spontaneous free-play of market forces*, the accidental results of numerous acts of buying and selling, behind which as a general tendency stands the law of value.

But alongside spontaneous control in society at any level of its development there is another type of control that is related to the purposeful activity of human beings. In this respect there have gradually been formed specific social institutions—the *subjects of control*; that is, the totality of organs and organisations that exert a conscious influence on the system with the intention of bringing about certain results. Most important among these organs are the state and the political parties.

The conscious factors of control in the course of social progress have undergone extensive changes—from control by tradition and custom, that is, from the experience gained and passed on from generation to generation which characterises primitive society, to the conscious control of society on a scientific basis as exists under socialism. The science-based management of Soviet society is carried out by the Soviet economic organisations and the public organisations led by the Communist Party.

Systems and the Environment

No *system* exists in isolation, but in interaction with other social and natural formations. These external (in relation to a given system) formations, with which a system is closely linked, form its *environment*. A living organism, for example, is indissolubly connected with the natural environment, the source of its nourishment.

The environment of a social system is extremely varied. It is primarily a *natural environment,* with which society interacts in terms of *material and energy sources.* A natural environment provides materials and energy for production and, on this basis, for organising social and cultural life. The environment for any social system consists of the other social systems with which it is in economic, social, cultural and informational interaction. In the case of Soviet society this environment consists of the other socialist countries, the developing countries and the capitalist countries.

The higher the organisation of the system, the more it is sensitive to the environment, on the one hand, and the more actively it influences the environment, on the other. An inanimate, inorganic system is destroyed and absorbed through interaction with its environment. A living organism on the whole adapts to it. Human beings and a social system not only retain their integrity in conditions of a changing environment, but also change the natural environment in conformity with their interests and needs.

The Dynamics of a System

"Dialectical logic," wrote Lenin, "requires that an object should be taken in development, in change, in 'self-movement'..."*

The scientific cognition of a system requires knowledge of how that system arose, of the main stages of its development, of its present condition and of its prospects. Furthermore, a new system does not arise immediately on the basis of the old. It does not appear in a ready-made form. It appears first in the form of certain preconditions, which often are the varied components of these other systems. In the emergence and development of systems, therefore, there is *continuity.*

The emergence of a new social system on the basis of those that preceded was convincingly explained by Marx, who analysed the development of the capitalist economic system, which arose within feudalism as a definite unity of the minimum of necessary components. These at first were capitalist manufactures and then large-scale machine production

---

* V.I. Lenin, *Collected Works 32*: 94.

together with commodity circulation and the conversion of labour power*
into a commodity. As a result of the bourgeois revolution, the capitalist
system replaced feudalism. It gradually but inexorably took over and
transformed, in accordance with its basic internal nature, all such economic forms as interest, commercial profit, rent and money. Further, it
created its special components, i.e., labour power as a commodity. Rent,
interest and commercial profit became components of the capitalist system
only when they had been brought into the general flow of the production
and accumulation of surplus value.

The components of a system, the elements of its structure, are not only
unequal from the point of view of their place and role in the functioning of
the system, but also from the point of view of their *prospective opportunities* for improvement and development. Some components lose their
importance in a system, others can never go beyond the framework of the
basic properties of the system and therefore have no future, others still
have great possibilities as the bearers of a new and better system, as the
preconditions for and embryo of its subsequent emergence. Therefore, the
study of a given system cannot be limited to examining its characteristics
purely from the point of view of their present condition. More important is
to reveal the *dynamics of a system* so as to discover among the variety of its
components those that are progressive and continually grow and develop,
for it is these that will determine the future.

In this respect Marx's and Engels's analysis of the complex system of
class relations in capitalist society remains a classical one. Revealing the
existence in this system of an advanced and progressive class—the proletariat, its great historic mission as the gravedigger of the bourgeoisie and
the creator of a new, socialist society, they showed the way forward for
humanity from capitalism to socialism.

An examination of the laws and categories of Marxist dialectics has
given us an idea of universal development and connections of the material
world. Our task now is to ascertain how this material world is cognised by
human beings. For this we have to study the theory of knowledge of dialectical materialism.

---

* The worker's ability to work.

CHAPTER VIII

The Theory of Knowledge of Dialectical Materialism

Dialectical materialism takes account of the wealth of experience accumulated by mankind and the greatest achievements of science and revolutionary practice, and on this basis concludes that the world is fully knowable and that man through his reason is capable of forming a correct idea of material reality.

Let us examine in detail the process of cognition of the world.

1. What Is Knowledge?

Knowledge is active, purposive reflection of the objective world and its laws in man's mind. The source of knowledge is the outside world around man. It acts on man and arouses in him corresponding sensations, ideas and concepts. Man sees forests, fields and mountains, feels the heat and sees the light of the sun, hears the singing of birds, smells the scent of flowers. If these objects existing outside of man's consciousness did not act on him, he would not have the least idea about them. It should be noted that man not only perceives objects and phenomena of the world, but *actively, practically,* acts upon them. We shall examine how he does this in more detail further on in the book.

The Marxist theory of knowledge is based on recognition of the objective world, its objects and phenomena a the *sole source* of human knowledge.

Idealists do not consider objective reality the source of our knowledge. In idealist philosophy the object of knowledge is either consciousness, sensation of the individual man (subject) or some kind of a mystic consciousness which is supposed to exist independent of man (take "absolute idea", "universal spirit", etc.).

A serious blow at idealism was struck by pre-Marxist materialists who regarded knowledge as a reflection of external objects in man's mind. But their ideas on the process of knowledge were also limited. Being metaphysicians they were unable to apply dialectics to the process of knowledge. They regarded reflection as a passive imprint of a thing on man's brain, comparing the latter with wax upon which things leave their imprint. Pre-Marxist materialists took no account of the activity, the life of man engaged in cognition. Moreover, their chief limitation lay in their failure to evaluate the role of practice in knowledge.

Marx and Engels went beyond the limits set by preceding philosophies in understanding the cognitive process and created a qualitatively new, *dialectical-materialist theory of knowledge*.

The fundamental distinction of the Marxist theory of knowledge is that it *bases the process of cognition on practice, the material, production activities of people*. It is in the course of this activity that man comes to know objects and phenomena. In Marxist philosophy practice is both the point of departure, the basis of the process of knowledge, and the criterion of truth, of correctness of knowledge. "The standpoint of life, of practice, should be first and fundamental in the theory of knowledge. And it inevitably leads to materialism,"* Lenin wrote.

It is in practice, in the material productive activity of people that knowledge manifests its activity, its purposeful nature. Man actively influences the world in the course of practice not all by himself, but together with other people, with society as a whole. And this means that if the *object* of knowledge, its source, is the material world, then the *subject* of knowledge and its carrier is the human society. Recognition of the *social nature* of knowledge is a key distinctive feature of the Marxist theory of knowledge.

The founders of Marxism discovered the *dialectics* of knowledge. From the point of view of dialectical materialism knowledge is an endless process of approximation of thought to the cognised object, the movement of thought from ignorance to knowledge, from incomplete, inexact knowledge to more complete and more exact. Replacing obsolete theories with new ones, rendering old theories more exact, knowledge marches onward, revealing ever new sides of reality.

Inasmuch as practice serves as the basis of knowledge, let us examine it and the role it plays in the cognitive process.

2. Practice—Starting Point and Basis of the Process of Knowledge

Practice is the active work of people in transforming nature and society. The basis of practice is labour, material production. Practice also includes the political side of life, the class struggle, the national liberation movement and scientific experience, experiments. Practice is social in character.

---

* V.I. Lenin, "Materialism and Empirio-Criticism", *Collected Works*, Vol. 14, p. 142.

It is, above all, the activity of large groups of people, of all working people, the producers of material wealth, and not of isolated individuals.

In the course of practice man not only transforms objects existing in nature, but also creates objects which are not available in ready-made form in nature. Man produces many artificial materials which at times surpass anything known to nature in durability and other important properties.

Practice is the *starting point and basis* of knowledge. Why? First of all because knowledge itself arose on the basis of practice, chiefly under the influence of material production. From the very first steps of his existence man had to work, to win his means of livelihood. In the process of work he came up against the forces of nature and by transforming them and making them serve his needs he gradually came to understand them. The further development of production demanded new knowledge. Even in antiquity man was faced with the need to measure land areas, to count the number of tools and the products he made. As a result, the first rudiments of mathematics appeared. Man built dwellings, bridges, roads, irrigation systems and other structures which called for the knowledge of mechanics. Thus, under the influence of practical requirements his cognitive abilities gradually developed and gave birth to science. Practice was also behind the birth of the social sciences. Marxism itself, as we know, arose on the foundation of the proletariat's revolutionary struggle.

Practice sets knowledge definite tasks and facilitates their accomplishment, thus advancing knowledge. The experience of socialist production in the Soviet Union, it was noted at the 25th CPSU Congress, shows that it is necessary to conduct research in the first place in areas which have a direct bearing on the all-round development of production and its management, and to draw up recommendations aimed at substantially raising the effectivity of production. This is the main task of Soviet economists.

Finally, practice provides instruments and equipment for scientific cognition and thereby facilitates the progress of knowledge. Without superpowerful particle accelerators and other very intricate scientific instruments and installations produced by modern industry, scientists would not have been able to discover the secrets of the atomic nucleus. We cannot imagine science today without electronic microscopes, space rockets and many other simple and complex instruments of knowledge. All these instruments are in fact the product of the material, practical activities of people.

Practice is not only the basis, but also the *aim* of knowledge. Man studies the surrounding world and learns the laws of its development in order to utilise the results of knowledge in his practical activities. It is true that these results are not always applied at once. The disintegration of the atom, for example, was discovered over 80 years ago, but it was only recently that man learned how to use atomic energy for practical purposes. And although often decades pass before scientific discoveries are applied, they are all determined, brought into being by the requirements of life.

Unity of Theory and Practice

Cognition is one of the forms of people's activity—it is their *theoretical* activity. But theory in itself is incapable of changing reality and this sets it apart from practice. Theory only reflects the world, generalises mankind's practical activity. But, while generalising practice, theory exerts a reverse influence upon it, contributes to its development. Theory without practice is pointless, practice without theory is blind. Theory indicates the way and helps to find the most efficient means of achieving practical objectives.

Let us take, for example, natural science. It has arisen on the basis of practice, as a result of the generalisation of people's production experience but at the same time it renders valuable assistance to production. It helps discover new methods of production, create highly efficient machinery and equipment, artificial raw and other materials, and so on.

Marxist-Leninist theory is very important for society's development. Being a correct, deep reflection of reality, a generalisation of the proletariat's revolutionary struggle, it guides the proletariat in its struggle for socialism and communism. What makes Marxism-Leninism viable is that it is true and, by revealing the true laws of social development, it enables Communist parties not only to act correctly today, but also to foresee the future, to scientifically plan practical activities for many years ahead. The Communist Party regards it as its sacred duty to further develop Marxist-Leninist theory, investigate the general laws of mature socialism and continue to promote the process of world development.

Unity of theory and practice is the supreme principle of Marxism-Leninism. This principle has acquired particularly great significance at the present time when cadres have to keep raising their knowledge of theory, Marxism-Leninism and skills and efficiency, when the complex problems relating to economic and social management should be dealt with promptly. Therefore, theory must continue to pave the way for practice and ensure a strictly scientific approach to the management of the economy and cultural life of the Soviet people.

3. From Living Perception to Abstract Thought

Knowledge does not stand still, but constantly moves and develops. This development of knowledge is expressed in its movement from direct living perception to abstract thought. "From living perception to abstract thought, and *from this to practice*,—such is the dialectical path of the cognition of the *truth*,"* Lenin wrote.

Sensory Knowledge

Knowledge always begins with a study of objects of the outside world with the aid of our sense organs. This we know from our day-to-day experience. If we want to study an unfamiliar object, we first of all carefully examine it, and, if need be, touch it with our fingers, taste it, etc. Direct perception of things is the initial phase, the first step on the road to knowledge. Man, on coming into contact with objects and phenomena of nature in the course of his practical activity, gains his first impressions of these objects and phenomena through his sense organs. The sense organs are a kind of a window through which the outside world "penetrates" man's consciousness and which enables him to perceive the colours, odours, and sounds of nature, the taste of its fruits, etc.

Sensation is the main form of sensory knowledge. *Sensation* is a reflection of individual properties, distinctions or sides of an object. Objects can be hot or cold, dark or light, smooth or rough—all these and many other properties, acting on our sense organs, arouse certain sensations.

Man's organism possesses a corresponding physiological apparatus for the formation of sensations. This apparatus consists, firstly, of sense organs, secondly, of nerve fibres through which, just like electricity along wires, excitation is transmitted to the respective parts of the cerebrum and, thirdly, of the sections of the brain where the excitations are transformed into corresponding sensations. Excitation caused by a definite sound in man's ear is transformed into the sensation of sound, while the action of light on the eye is transformed into the sensation of light, and so on.

What makes sensations tremendously important in the process of cognition is that they provide material enabling us to judge an object. The entire subsequent process of knowledge rests on the information about objects which sensations give us.

* V.I. Lenin, "Conspectus of Hegel's Book *The Science of Logic*", *Collected Works*, Vol. 38, p. 171.

Lenin defined sensation as a *subjective image of the objective world*. This means that sensation, being a reflection of objectively existing objects, is not their mechanical imprint on man's brain, but an *ideal image*. This image is *subjective* because it belongs to man (subject) and to humanity, and not to the outside world. This means that the nature of sensation is influenced in a certain way by the specific features of the psyche, the individual qualities of the given person, and above all by social conditions, by his social environment.

One of the main indications of the subjective nature of sensations is the fact that people differently perceive identical outside influences.

Does this mean then that sense organs give us an incorrect idea of the world? No, it does not. Daily experience and scientific data prove that sense organs do not deceive us. If the indications of one sense organ arouse doubts, we turn to the others. If a man does not believe his own eyes, he resorts to the use of his fingers, and if this is not enough, he has at his service the eyes and fingers of other people. If, lastly, even this is not enough, man turns to instruments, experiments, practical experience. Thus, sense organs, checked by each other, by the sensations of other people, by experience, experiment and practice, give us, on the whole, a correct idea of things accessible to us.

In addition to sensations, sensory knowledge consists of perceptions and ideas. *Perception* is a higher form of sensory knowledge. It reflects an object in its sensory, direct entirety, the total of its external aspects and distinctive features. An *idea* is the reproduction in man's mind of earlier perceptions. We, for example, can reproduce in our mind, can bring to mind the image of our teacher, although we may not have seen him for many years.

Logical Knowledge

The picture given by sense organs is uncommonly rich and colourful. It is, however, limited and far from complete. Sensory knowledge gives us an idea only of external aspects of things. With the aid of sense organs, for example, it is possible to perceive an electric bulb but it is impossible to imagine that electricity is a stream of electrons moving at a certain velocity. Nor is it possible to perceive, through sense organs, the tremendous velocity of light, the movement of elementary particles in the atom and many other complex phenomena of nature and social life.

In a word, sensory knowledge cannot reveal the inner nature of things, their essence, the laws of their development. Yet this is the main purpose of knowledge. Only knowledge of laws, of the essence of things can serve man as a guide in his practical activity. It is here that abstract or, as it is also called, logical thought comes to his aid.

Logical thought is a qualitatively new, higher stage in the development of knowledge. Its role is to reveal an object's chief properties and features. It is at the stage of logical thought that man gains knowledge of the laws governing the development of reality, so needed for his practical activity.

Concept is the main form of logical thought. A *concept* reflects in objects not all their aspects, but only what is *essential* and *general;* it abstracts, casts aside secondary features. Let us consider, for example, the concept "man". Not all the features of an individual are reflected in this concept. It contains no information about nationality, age, place of residence, the time when he lives, and so on. Fixed in this concept is only what is general and essential, inherent in everyone—the ability to work, to produce material wealth, to think and to speak. Similarly, the concepts "tree", "animal", "society", "production", "class", "party", etc., cover what is general and essential in objects.

Concepts arise on the basis of practice. Before forming, for example, the concepts of triangle, square and other geometric figures, man in his practical activities came into contact with numerous objectively existing triangular, square and other objects. Practice is the basis of the generalising activity of the mind, the processing of the data furnished by sensory knowledge. As man acted upon the objects of the material world, he compared them and, abstracting from everything accidental and secondary, singled out what was general and essential in them, and ascertained their objective importance in the process of production and their place in man's labour and life. It is the continuous process of creative work and man's ceaseless efforts to make nature serve him and the interests of production that gave rise to scientific concepts such as "electric power", "atomic energy", "hybridisation", "melioration" and many, many others.

At first glance it might seem that concepts or abstractions are poorer than direct sense perceptions. But, Lenin noted, even the simplest concept reflects nature more deeply, fully and truly because it reflects the internal aspects of reality inaccessible to direct sensory cognition. It reflects nature more fully, because it covers not one object or small group of objects, but their mass, their boundless multitude.

The transition from the sensory to the abstract represents a dialectical leap in the process of knowledge, in its movement from the lower to the higher. This leap is made through practice. Only the practical activity of people, aimed at transforming objects and phenomena of the world, makes it possible to penetrate their essence, to differentiate between the important and the secondary, the internal and the external. The higher the degree of development of practical activity, and the more powerful its transforming force, the deeper and more diverse is the knowledge of man.

Concepts reflect the changing world, the constantly developing practice, and hence they themselves must be *flexible* and *mobile*. Mobility and flexibility of concepts is expressed in the amplification and deepening of existing concepts and also in the formation of new ones corresponding to the changed objective conditions, the changed practice.

Other forms of thought—judgements and conclusions—are formed on the basis of concepts.

Judgement is a form of thought in which something is asserted (for example, "socialism is peace") or something is denied (for example, "Marxism is not a dogma"). As we see, a judgement consists of definite concepts. In the judgements given above these are the concepts "socialism", "peace", "Marxism", and "dogma". At the same time it is impossible to understand these concepts without other judgements, such as "socialism is a social system based on public ownership", etc. Concepts and judgements are thus interconnected. Judgements are also interconnected. Their connection makes up a special form of logical thought—conclusion. A *conclusion* is a new judgement obtained on the basis of other judgements (premises). Through conclusions drawn from available knowledge we can gain new knowledge, and this is what makes for their great importance in cognition. Such higher forms of knowledge as hypothesis and theory represent an intricate combination of concepts, judgements and conclusions. A *hypothesis* is an assumption about phenomena, events, laws. The assumptions about the origin of life on Earth or the origin of the solar system are examples of hypotheses. *Scientific theories* embody deep, all-round knowledge of definite processes or fields of activity. This type of knowledge has been tested by experiment and practice. For example, the modern theory of the atomic nucleus, the theory of relativity in physics, and the materialist theory of heredity in biology are all scientific theories. Historical materialism is the truly scientific theory of the development of society.

Thus, we see that knowledge in its dialectical development traverses a long road, from the simplest sensations to complex scientific theories.

This picture of the formation of scientific theories constitutes only a general trend in the dialectical-materialist process of knowledge. In reality it often happens that under the influence of practical needs the researcher first conceives an *idea* which foreshadows the movement of thought and indicates the main directions of scientific study. At times this idea provides only a very vague, approximate response to demands posed by practice. In the course of the realisation of the idea and in the process of investigation concepts, images and judgements arise that concretise the idea, embody it in the flesh of scientific premises, conclusions, and laws which after passing the test of practice turn in their totality and unity into scientific theory.

It should be noted that the idea which foreshadows theory is born not only under the impact of practice; it is also dictated by the *logical development of science itself*. And in both cases the idea is not simply the fruit of its author's imagination. Accumulating, as it does, the already available knowledge, it is in its way a result of the development of science and practice. An immense role in the formation of ideas and their realisation and development into a scientific theory is played by the scientist, by his experience, knowledge, intuition, imagination and creative abilities.

Unity of the Sensory and the Logical in Knowledge

Sensory knowledge and abstract thought represent a *unity:* they reflect one and the same material world and have a common basis: the practical activity of mankind. Both these stages of knowledge have one physiological basis, man's nervous system.

Abstract thought is impossible without sensory knowledge inasmuch as the information furnished by the sense organs is the sole material for forming concepts. There can be nothing in thought that is not given to man by his sense organs. But, having arisen on the basis of sensations, abstract thought goes deeper than sensory knowledge, enriches and extends its bounds. Sensory impressions, illumined by the light of reason, acquire new content.

Since the sensory and the logical act in unity, supplementing and enriching each other, neither the indications of the sensations nor the conclusions of reason must be ignored in the process of cognition. Yet there are trends in philosophy which understand the process of knowledge one-sidedly.

Supporters of *empiricism* (from the Greek *empeiria,* meaning experience) underestimate the role of abstract thought in knowledge, maintaining that sense impressions alone give man a true picture of the world. Since concepts cannot be perceived by the senses (it is impossible, for example, to imagine a "man in general", a "tree in general", and so on), empiricists claim that in reality nothing corresponds to concepts, that they are the product of man's imagination.

Empiricism is widespread in modern bourgeois philosophy and sociology. This is not surprising. Bourgeois ideologists fear broad generalisations and are anxious to avoid solutions of concrete social problems and withdraw into the realm of insignificant facts and superficial observations.

In contrast to empiricists, supporters of *rationalism* do not trust the sense organs and consider reason, abstract thought the sole source of true knowledge. Rationalists underestimate the role of sensory knowledge and assume that man is capable of cognising the world intuitively, without any experience. By divorcing concepts and other forms of thought from sensations and perceptions, rationalists ultimately lapse into idealism.

It follows that logical knowledge must not be divorced from sensory knowledge because this inevitably leads to a distortion of the cognitive process, to the divorce of thought from reality; this is typical of all trends of idealism. Idealism has certain gnosiological* and class roots which account for its tenacity. Let us examine these roots.

Gnosiological and Class Roots of Idealism

It is the *one-sided exaggeration, absolutisation* of the aspects of the most complex process of knowledge, their divorce from reality, from the objective world, that make up the gnosiological roots of idealism.

Lenin called idealism a sterile flower, but a sterile flower that is not groundless, but grows on the living tree of fertile and powerful human knowledge. The gnosiological roots of idealism are contained *within the process of knowledge itself* which, as we have seen, is uncommonly complex and contradictory.

Knowledge possesses the possibility of deviation, divorce of thought from the cognised object, from reality. This deviation can be seen in the simplest concepts which man uses all the time, such, for example, as a "house in general", a "table in general". In reality there is neither a "house in general" nor a "table in general", but only definite houses, definite tables. The concepts "house" and "table", as we know, single out only the general essential features which all houses and all tables have. The moment we forget that concepts have their source in real objects and divorce them from reality, we can imagine that they have arisen and exist of themselves, independently of the object. This is idealism.

This is how objective idealism arose. Its supporters hold that the concept exists independently of the object, "creates" this object. On the other hand, subjective idealists, proceeding from sensations as the direct source of our

---

* Gnosiology (from the Greek *gnosis*—knowledge, and *logos*—word) is the science of knowledge, the theory of knowledge.

knowledge, declare that the only thing that exists is these sensations, and regard objects and phenomena as the sum-total of sensations.

Thus, rectilinearity and one-sidedness, subjectivism and subjective blindness are, according to Lenin, the gnosiological roots of idealism.

It should be noted, however, that the gnosiological roots create only the prerequisites, the possibility for idealism to exist and that definite social forces turn this possibility into reality. These forces are the reactionary classes interested in a perversion of the truth. It is their class interests that cause them to consolidate the subjectivist, one-sided approach to knowledge, the divorce of thought from reality.

The spread of idealism is also facilitated by the antithesis between mental and manual labour which exists in an antagonistic class society and gives rise to a seeming independence of the consciousness of men from their material, productive activity. Their monopoly of mental labour enables the exploiting classes to propagate and support idealism in every way and utilise it to justify and maintain their rule.

Idealism has not only gnosiological roots, but also *class roots*—the definite interests of the reactionary classes.

And so, knowledge develops from the sensory to the logical through practice. The results of knowledge naturally have to be verified; it is necessary to ascertain whether they are true. It could not be otherwise as only true knowledge can serve the practical requirements of people.

Before describing how the results of knowledge are tested, how truth is reached, let us examine truth.

4. The Marxist Theory of Truth

Objectivity of Truth

Dialectical materialism understands *truth* as that knowledge of an object which *correctly* reflects this object, i.e., *corresponds* to it. For example, the scientific propositions that "bodies consist of atoms", that the "Earth existed prior to man", that "the people are the makers of history", etc., are true.

On what does truth depend? Does it depend on man, in whose mind this truth arises, or on the object it reflects?

Idealists hold that truth is subjective, that it depends on man who himself determines the truth of his knowledge without regard for the real state of affairs.

In contrast to idealism, dialectical materialism, relying on scientific discoveries and man's age-long practical experience, maintains that truth is *objective*. Since truth reflects the objectively existing world, its content does not depend on man's consciousness. Objective truth, Lenin wrote, is the content of our knowledge which depends neither on man nor on mankind. The content of truth is fully determined by the objective processes it reflects.

Let us consider, for example, the statement: "The Earth is shaped like a sphere." This assertion is true inasmuch as it corresponds to reality. But does the shape of the Earth depend on man's consciousness? Not in the least; the Earth existed long before man, and its spherical form was shaped by natural forces. Examining any other truth, we arrive at a similar conclusion.

From Relative to Absolute Truth

Recognising the objectivity of truth, dialectical materialism also solves another important problem of knowledge: *how* man cognises objective truth—at once, as a whole, unconditionally, absolutely or only approximately, relatively. This question concerns the relationship of absolute to relative truth.

The distinctions between absolute and relative truth are determined by the varying *degree of correspondence* of man's knowledge to reality. Some knowledge fully corresponds to reality, with absolute exactness, other knowledge only partially. *Absolute truth* is objective truth in its entirety, an absolutely exact reflection of reality.

Is it possible to cognise absolute truth in its entirety? In principle, yes, since, on the one hand, nothing is unknowable while, on the other, there are no bounds to the cognitive abilities of the human mind.

An individual, or a particular generation of people, however, is limited in knowledge by the corresponding historical conditions, the level of development of production, science and experimental techniques. That is why man's knowledge at each stage of history is relative; it inevitably assumes the character of relative truth. *Relative truth* is the incomplete correspondence of knowledge to reality. Lenin called this truth the *relatively true* reflection of an object which is independent of man. Corresponding to reality in essence, this knowledge needs to be further specified, deepened and tested in practice.

That being the case, perhaps absolute truth is not knowable at all? No, that is not so. True, it is impossible to cognise absolute truth at once, in its entirety, for it can only be reached in the endless process of knowledge.

With each new achievement of science man draws closer to the cognition of absolute truth, to knowing its new elements, links and sides. Knowledge progresses because man, by cognising relative truths, cognises absolute truth as well.

Let us take as an example the modern theory of the atom. In the main, it corresponds to reality, but as a whole it is, nevertheless, relative truth. We cannot say that man knows absolutely everything about the atom. So many secrets are still hidden in the atom that it will take more than one generation of scientists to uncover them. Science has to solve the very intricate problem of the internal structure of elementary particles which make up the atom, the causes of their changes, transmutations and many other problems. At the same time the atomic theory contains grains of absolute truth, of complete, absolutely exact knowledge; what science has learned about the existence of the atom, of its nucleus with tremendous latent reserves of energy and numerous mobile and variable particles, etc., is absolute, non-transient knowledge.

This means that relative truth must also contain grains of absolute truth. Man's knowledge is *both* absolute and relative: relative because it is not exhaustive and can be endlessly developed and deepened, revealing new sides of reality; absolute, because it contains elements of eternal, absolutely exact knowledge.

Man has gained many ideas about individual sides of reality which are of a non-transient, absolute character. Such, for example, are the propositions of Marxist philosophy: "matter is primary, consciousness is secondary", "consciousness is a property of the brain", the law of conservation and transformation of energy and other laws and conclusions of the natural and social sciences. The fundamental theses of Marxist-Leninist theory, whose correctness has been confirmed by practice, are absolute truth. Although Marxist-Leninist theory is constantly developing, its basic principles cannot be refuted.

"Human thought," Lenin wrote, "...by its nature is capable of giving, and does give, absolute truth, which is compounded of a sum-total of relative truths. Each step in the development of science adds new grains to the sum of absolute truth, but the limits of the truth of each scientific proposition are relative, now expanding, now shrinking with the growth of knowledge."*

More than half a century ago Lenin wrote that the human mind, which discovered so many wonders in nature, would discover much more and

---

* V.I. Lenin, "Materialism and Empirio-Criticism", *Collected Works*, Vol. 14, p. 135.

thus increase its power over it. What a striking confirmation of his profound predictions are the achievements of modern science, including Soviet science.

Man has penetrated the innermost depths of the atom and has placed its mighty, truly inexhaustible forces at his service. The harnessed atom generates electricity, turns the propeller shafts of atomic ships, helps in the treatment of diseases and performs many other useful services.

Man is gradually extending his power over the boundless expanse of the Universe. Through his reason he penetrates matter deeply and extensively, discovering new secrets of outer space. Not so long ago it was thought that outer space is a void illuminated only by the faint light of distant stars and penetrated by rare meteorites. Now, as a result of space research, we know that the Earth is girded by belts of charged particles. Information has been received about the upper layers of the atmosphere, their composition and density, cosmic rays and micro-meteorites, the tiny particles of interplanetary substance.

Mankind's age-old dream, the exploration of the Cosmos, is now being realised. Mars, Venus, Saturn and other planets of the solar system and their satellites, including the Moon, the satellite of the Earth, are being studied. Space exploration is already adding new invaluable grains of knowledge to the infinite sum comprising the absolute truth.

Concreteness of Truth

According to dialectical materialism, truth gained in the process of knowledge is always related to a definite, concrete sphere of reality which likewise develops in definite conditions. There is no abstract truth, *truth is always concrete.*

Is classical mechanics, for example, true? Yes, it is true, but only in definite, concrete spheres of reality, not in all of them. It correctly reflects the movement of macroscopic bodies, but loses its true character in the microworld. The new, quantum mechanics is true here. And this is the case with any other truth: while correctly reflecting certain concrete phenomena, it is unable to reflect others correctly.

Even for one and the same process, however, truth cannot be eternal or fixed once and for all. This process itself develops, the conditions in which it takes place change and naturally the truth reflecting it also undergoes change. What was true in certain conditions may become untrue in other changed conditions.

The principle that truth is concrete is particularly important in the present-day situation for the successful struggle of the peoples for peace, democracy, national liberation and socialism. This principle demands, above all, a correct understanding of the contemporary epoch. The main content of our epoch is the transition from capitalism to socialism, when the world socialist system is turning into the decisive factor of mankind's development. It is on the basis of these fundamental characteristics of our epoch that Marxist parties solve the fundamental issues of our time, about prospects of the struggle against capitalism and for socialism, and the ways and means of pursuing it, about war and peace, etc.

Let us take such a cardinal issue of our age as the question of war and peace.

An analysis of the reactionary essence of imperialism brought Lenin to the conclusion that under imperialism wars are inevitable. He based his conclusion on the existing situation: the imperialists ruled the world, had divided it among themselves and were engaged in a relentless battle for its re-division. In Lenin's lifetime there was no world socialist system, but even then he predicted that mankind would inevitably be faced with the historic task of turning the dictatorship of the proletariat from a national phenomenon existing in one country into an international one, into a dictatorship of the proletariat existing in at least several advanced countries and capable of exerting influence on all world development.

Lenin called for a dialectical approach to the question of wars, i.e., for strict account of the concrete historical situation and changes in the balance of forces in the world. This correlation of forces has now radically changed in favour of peace and socialism. A world socialist system has arisen and is vigorously developing, there is a widespread movement of the people for peace, headed by the working class, the most implacable foe of aggressive wars, and the number of peace-loving non-socialist states is growing. All this taken together has given the Communist Party of the Soviet Union and other Marxist parties grounds for concluding that at present war is not fatally inevitable and that conditions exist for preventing war.

Dogmatists and sectarians are attacking this creative, genuinely Marxist solution of the problem of war and peace. They ignore the new conditions and cling to obsolete conclusions and propositions. Divorced from concrete reality, refusing to see the new correlation of forces in the world, they declare that today, too, wars are inevitable. By denying the possibility of preventing another world war, dogmatists thereby exert a demoralising influence on the working people. Indeed, is it worth building a new life, if it will be later consumed in the flames of an atomic war?

Yet the assertion that wars are no longer fatally inevitable does not mean that every possibility of war has been removed: imperialism is still a permanent threat to peace and social progress. Hence the need for an active struggle of the peoples against the danger of war, and for stronger unity of all peace-loving forces.

Marxist-Leninist parties condemn dogmatism and sectarianism, and in all their multifarious activities consistently apply the principle of a concrete historical approach to reality.

In its internal and foreign policy the CPSU never fails to reckon with concrete historical conditions, the changing objective possibilities, the level of economic development and other social factors. It was with account for concrete historical conditions that the party carried out important measures which ensured the victory of socialism in the USSR (transition to a new economic policy, NEP, industrialisation and so forth). It is with account for internal conditions and the international situation that plans for perfecting a developed socialist society are being drawn up and implemented.

5. Practice—Criterion of Truth

To find a criterion of truth is to find the objective basis which does not depend on man and makes it possible to distinguish truth, true knowledge, from delusion.

Practice is the sole criterion of truth. We can argue as much as we like about the true character of any idea or scientific theory, but this dispute can only be settled by practice, i.e., in economic production, political life or scientific experiment. "The question whether objective truth can be attributed to human thinking is not a question of theory but is a *practical* question," Marx wrote. "Man must prove the truth, i.e. the reality and power, the this-worldliness of his thinking in practice."*

Idealists of all kinds disagree with this important proposition of dialectical materialism. They deny the importance of practice in knowledge and maintain that man himself, his thought, is the criterion of truth. What is useful, what is beneficial is true—this idea is asserted, for example, by *pragmatists,* representatives of a trend in idealist philosophy which is especially widespread in the United States. Such an understanding of truth leads pragmatists to justify the reactionary actions of contemporary capitalism. Since the exploitation of the workers, imperialist wars and plunder of less developed countries are of benefit, and bring profit to the capitalists, they are, from the pragmatists' viewpoint, true and natural.

* Karl Marx, "Theses on Feuerbach", in: Karl Marx, Frederick Engels, *Collected Works,* Vol. 5, p. 3.

Usefulness, however, cannot serve as a criterion of truth. On the contrary, only true knowledge brings benefit to mankind. Man can rely in his practical work only on true correct knowledge; only truth can bring him the results he expects. Therefore, if man, acting on the knowledge gained, reaches during his practical activity the aim he set himself, obtains the expected results, this signifies that his knowledge corresponds to reality, is true.

Here is one example. More than half a century ago, the Russian scientist Konstantin Tsiolkovsky developed the scientific theory of rocketry. He expressed the unusually bold idea, a truly fantastic idea at that time, that rockets could be used for flights to other celestial bodies. "Man will take a rock from the Moon," Tsiolkovsky wrote.

It took a great deal of effort to turn Tsiolkovsky's brilliant ideas into reality. The first artificial satellite of the Earth was launched from a Soviet cosmodrome; Yuri Gagarin's first orbital flight, and the flight of Soviet and U.S. space stations paved the way for the first landing on the Moon of a piloted spaceship on July 20, 1969. Several hours after the landing Neil Armstrong and Edwin Aldrin set foot on the lunar surface and took the first samples of moonrock and dust. This was practical confirmation of Tsiolkovsky's ideas, ideas that had seemed fantastic in their time.

Social theories and ideas, too, are tested in practice, in the revolutionary struggle of classes, the political activities of states, of various parties, and in the struggle of the peoples for peace and progress. The truth of the Marxist-Leninist theory is being confirmed by life itself, by the practical activities of the international working-class and communist movement and by the struggle of the imperialist-oppressed peoples for national and social liberation. The irrepressible movement of mankind from capitalism to socialism offers incontrovertible proof of the great vital force, the great truth of the Marxist-Leninist teaching.

6. Means and Methods of Scientific Cognition

The purpose of scientific cognition is to ascertain the inner nature, the essence of objects and phenomena, and the laws governing their functions and development. But essence and laws do not lie on the surface of phenomena. In order to discover them a range of means and methods of scientific cognition have been elaborated in the course of the long and complex development of science and practice. These means and methods are of universal significance and can be applied in all sciences investigating the most diverse phenomena of reality.

What are the means and methods of scientific cognition?

Observation and Experiment

One of the most widespread methods of scientific cognition, especially in natural science, is *scientific observation,* a purposeful contemplation and perception of objects and phenomena in their natural state, i.e., such as they are in reality. The results of observation depend on the extent of the researcher's preliminary knowledge of the object which he studies, on his ability correctly to formulate the purpose of his investigation and his determination to achieve his aim, and his skill to give a faithful and exhaustive description of the results obtained.

As distinct from observation, an *experiment* is investigation of an object that is placed in artificial, carefully considered conditions. This makes it possible to fix and study the object in its pure form and to ascertain how the object as a whole and its individual aspects change under the influence of specific conditions. For example, having obtained one or another chemical substance in its pure form, a chemist studies its properties and finds out how they change under the influence of temperature, humidity, pressure and other factors.

Experiment is one of the most important methods of cognition. It is broadly employed in natural science and is steadily gaining in importance in social sciences. There are all kinds of experiments ranging from small laboratory tests to vast production ones. Today, when science is becoming a direct productive force, production is turning into a huge experimental field where scientific discoveries, new machines and technology, and new scientific methods of the organisation of labour and management are put to severe and all-round tests.

The Role of Instruments in Scientific Cognition

People conduct observations and experiments mainly with the help of their sense organs. But the perceptive powers of these organs are limited. For instance, a naked eye can discern an object which is not smaller than one-fortieth of a millimetre. The limited capacity of the sense organs is augmented by *instruments* without which science, particularly modern science, is inconceivable. The modern electronic microscope, for instance, enlarges the image of objects millions of times, and an analytical balance measures "weights" as small as one millionth of a milligram.

Science employs the most diverse instruments. Above all they are *means of making measurements and observations*—chronometers, telescopes, microscopes, voltmeters, amperemeters, analytical balances, seismographs, the Wilson chamber (for studying elementary particles) and others; they are *recording devices:* photographic equipment, microfilms, memory tapes, control clocks and so forth; they are *communications means*—telegraph, telephone, radio, television, radars, photoelements, dictaphones, signalling devices, etc; finally, they are *computers*— arithmometers, slide rules, electronic computers, mathematical tables, and so forth.

An especially great role in modern science is played by computers which enormously broaden man's intellectual capacity and rid him of the need to perform tedious operations (calculations, search for necessary data and so forth). Computers are a very powerful means of gathering, storing and processing information whose volume in our day of the scientific and technical revolution is increasing at an exceptionally rapid pace.

Instruments are indispensable for studying microprocesses which cannot be directly perceived. At the same time they have a "disturbing" effect on the object of investigation. For instance, in a certain way they change, or modify the properties of elementary particles. This provides idealists with the pretext to deny the objective reality of microparticles and to assert that their properties are created by instruments in the course of observation and measurement. But the fact that one and the same property can be observed with the help of different instruments, and that with the help of one instrument it is possible to observe various properties of particles, shows that the idealistic view of the microcosm is untenable. Nevertheless, when investigating the microcosm it is important to take the influence of the instruments into account, to segregate this influence and pick out the objective properties of the particles in their more or less "pure" state.

Analysis and Synthesis

Any object is a totality (a system) of various interacting components, characteristics and aspects. What has to be done to determine the intricately linked components of an object and find out its essence? An important role in the investigation of such systems is played by analysis. *Analysis* is the breaking up of an object into its fundamental elements in order to ascertain their place and pick out the most essential ones. Analysis, Lenin wrote, is "separation of components", a division of the given concrete phenomenon. There can be a factual analysis and a logical analysis. The *factual analysis* is mainly used to investigate inorganic nature. For instance, a chemical analysis divides a molecule into its components—atoms, ions and radicals. If, for certain reasons, the object cannot be destroyed then *logical analysis* is used. It is most widely employed in studying living organisms and social systems. Only the analytical activity of thought can disclose the diversity and complexity of a socio-economic formation, class, nation and other social phenomena.

As distinct from analysis, *synthesis* is the material or mental combination of an object's components and aspects with the view to determining their inner, essential links and consequently its inherent laws. Chemists, for instance, synthesise molecules out of atoms, radicals and ions, and study the laws of chemical motion. Sociologists mentally unite various aspects of the life of society and thus obtain a general idea of society.

Man acquired his aptitude for analytical and synthetical cognition in the course of practical activity. During his life and work man encountered numerous objects and phenomena which he divided into parts and united into various implements of labour, mechanisms and structures. Pondering the results of practical analysis and synthesis he gradually turned them into very efficient methods of scientific research.

Analysis and synthesis are a unity since the object and its components are also a unity. They are interacting aspects of a single analytical and synthetical method of scientific cognition. Marx, investigating in his *Capital* the capitalist mode of production, at first broke it up into its components (production proper, circulation, distribution, etc.) and studied them. After that he united all these components and acquired a thorough knowledge of capitalism as a whole. As a result, he fathomed the secret of capitalist exploitation, disclosed the irreconcilable contradictions of capitalism and concluded that its doom was inevitable.

Induction and Deduction

Induction is an instance of reasoning from individual phenomena to general conclusions. Law, as we know, is general and is repeated in phenomena. But the general exists only in the individual. Since induction is a means of obtaining knowledge of the general from knowledge of the individual, it is an important method of cognising regularities, and causal relationships. Thus, on the basis of an infinite number of facts proving that one form of motion of matter turns into another form, and invariably without any loss of quantity, physicists discovered the fundamental law of nature—the law of conservation and transformation of energy.

Induction is a method of obtaining new knowledge because it helps to extend the already available knowledge to a range of new, still unstudied objects. But by extending knowledge about one class of objects to another and broader one, induction does not in the main alter the essence of knowledge. This attests to the limited nature of induction. Hence the need to supplement it with analysis, synthesis, generalisation and other methods of investigation.

Deduction is an instance of reasoning from the general to the individual. Given knowledge of a class of objects as a whole it is possible by means of deduction to extend this knowledge to any object of the same class. For instance, thanks to our knowledge of Mendeleyev's periodic law of chemical elements we can assert that the properties of any elements, whether known or still undiscovered, depend on the positive charge of its atomic nucleus.

Deduction is used as a means of formulating scientific theories. For example, contemporary science widely employs the *axiomatic* method when a scientific theory is built up in keeping with specific rules and laws drawn from the totality of axioms, i.e., propositions that are accepted without proof.

Induction and deduction, like analysis and synthesis, are a unity. Indeed, in order to cognise the general it is necessary to know the particular, and vice versa. Using induction and deduction as one, a researcher cognises reality as a unity of the particular and the general.

Historical and Logical Methods of Cognition

Each specific object, as we know, appears, develops and, finally, disappears to give place to the new. In other words, an object has its history. Celestial bodies, plants and animals, all have their history. Humanity also has a long history of development in the course of which it moved from the primitive to the socialist system. The history of humanity in its turn includes the histories of different socio-economic formations, continents and countries.

History is a maze of innumerable events: general and individual, necessary and accidental, major and secondary, etc. Historical processes are studied from different viewpoints and with the help of the different methods. One of them is a detailed study of history, of all its events. This is the *historical* method of investigation. Another method, the *logical* method is the study of the general, of what is repeated in the historical process. In essence the logical is the same as historical, but purged of the mass of details, of all that is accidental. Logical study, Engels wrote, is "nothing else but the reflection of the historical course in abstract and theoretically consistent form".*

The historical and logical methods are a unity, for they are used to study the appearance and development of one and the same object. Neglect of one and absolutisation of the other lead to serious errors in theory and practice. Disregard for the historical method causes a researcher to lapse into subjectivism, pointless theorisation and elaboration of logical constructions not connected with the actual historical process. A researcher who ignores the logical method interprets the historical process as a conglomeration of empirical facts devoid of unity and inner links. Being the logic of scientific cognition, Marxist dialectics examines phenomena and processes in their connection with other phenomena and processes, in their unity with concrete historical experience.

The Abstract and the Concrete

Another method of studying an object in its movement and development, of its inner relations is *ascendance from the abstract to the concrete.*

Abstraction is a result of mentally isolating certain aspects or properties of an object so as to attend to others, more important and essential at the given stage of investigation. This gives rise to abstract concepts which, as we know, are an important form of logical cognition.

The concrete, as distinct from the abstract, is the result of the fusion of concepts, which are obtained in the process of abstraction, into a single whole. The concrete is the reflection of the unity of the components, of the connections and relations of the object being cognised.

Since the abstract and the concrete are logical categories they rest on objective reality, on the unity, wholeness of objects and phenomena and on the existence of their components, sides and properties. Taking this into account, Marx viewed the cognition of an object as *movement of thought from the abstract to the concrete,* from simple, elementary concepts reproducing certain components or sides of an object, to more complex concepts and scientific theories and systems reproducing the object fully in its entire complexity.

Marx's *Capital* is a brilliant example of how scientific knowledge is acquired by means of ascending from the abstract to the concrete. Proceeding from the concept of commodity, the starting point of abstrac-

---

* Karl Marx, "Preface to *Contribution to the Critique of Political Economy"*, in: *Karl Marx and Frederick Engels, Selected Works* in three volumes, Volume One, p. 514. See also Marx/ Engels, *Collected Works 16*: p. 475.

tion characterising the essence of capitalist production, Marx went on to more and more abstractions (money, capital, surplus value, wages, etc.) and gradually recreated a complete picture of capitalist economy. As a result capitalist production appears as the concrete, as a "synthesis of many concepts", as "unity of multiformity".*

Nevertheless, all this does not repudiate an important premise of dialectical materialism that cognition begins with the sensory perception of an object. Prior to formulating abstract concepts and then synthesising them into a concrete whole, Marx scrupulously studied innumerable facts, aspects and features of capitalist reality which could be directly perceived. On the basis of these facts Marx formulated abstract concepts and then ascended from the abstract to the concrete.

Mathematical Methods

A distinguishing feature of modern science is the mounting *role of mathematical methods* in scientific research. Mathematics is widely applied in natural sciences and is penetrating social sciences.

It is common knowledge that all phenomena and processes have measure, unity of quantitative and qualitative features. Since qualities are manifested in properties that have quantitative gradations such as magnitude, level of development, etc., it is possible to use mathematics in investigating nature and society.

Mathematics has penetrated other sciences because it is highly abstract and has an extraordinary broad range of principles. And this is consistent with one of the main trends in the development of modern science—the growth of abstract knowledge. Today there are scientific trends which cannot be visually expressed and substantiated by laboratory experiments. But mathematics has a range of concepts (function, set, group, infinite set, etc.), which in terms of their breadth and universality are close to philosophical and thus make it possible to reflect the general quantitative characteristics of qualitatively different phenomena.

Moreover, mathematics has an exceptionally strict inner logic. If there are certain premises and if they are true, then owing to the inner logic of mathematics their corollaries are true.

Another reason why mathematics is penetrating other sciences is that the indices with which it operates are not necessarily numerical. It has a formi-

* Karl Marx, *Grundrisse der Kritik der Politischen Okonomie (Rohentwurf), 1857-1858*, Moscow, 1939, 218.

dable arsenal of means (models, matrices, functions, graphics, symbols, etc.), which alongside quantitative can also express certain qualitative features of objects and phenomena, and disclose their intricate relations and interdependence.

Yet it would be wrong to overestimate the role that mathematics can play. Mathematical methods produce results only when the qualitative nature, the essence of objects and phenomena are known. Hence the need for a close alliance of mathematics with other sciences.

Modelling

The *modelling* of objects and processes is becoming increasingly widespread in contemporary science. Objects and processes even of the most different kind are, in some respects, similar. For example, a geographical map and the terrain which it depicts are similar, and so is a photograph and the original.

Due to the similarity of various objects it is possible to model, i. e., to reproduce an object (system) with the help of another object which resembles it in some respects. The method of cognition which with the help of one system (natural and, more often than not, artificial or man-made) makes it possible to reproduce another, more complicated system that is the object of study is called *scientific modelling,* and the system which reproduces this object is called its *model.* Modelling is a simplified reproduction of the original, but this simplification should not be arbitrary and excessive, otherwise the model will not resemble the original, and no fresh knowledge about the original will be obtained.

There are two basic classes of models. *Material* models are material reproductions of objects which are being studied. Such, for example, are electronic models of the nervous system, the heart, kidneys and other organs and tissues of the living organism that are now used in biology and medicine. *Ideal* models are a totality of reasoning elements—mathematical and other formulas, equations, logical symbols, diverse signs, and so forth. An important place in the class of ideal models is occupied by *mathematical* models. The similarity of certain qualitative features in various objects makes it possible to investigate them with the help of the contemporary mathematics, particularly mathematical logic, the theory of probabilities, theory of sets and others, and also electronic computers.

A model is an effective means of scientific cognition. It comes to the assistance of the researcher when the object being investigated cannot be studied directly, because it is too big, too massive or too far away; because it has excessively high or low temperatures and pressures, and toxic or other properties harmful to man; because its direct study may violate its function and even destroy it, and so forth.

Another merit of modelling is that with its help it is possible to study objects which do not exist as yet, or which are to be created. First a model is made and then, after it undergoes theoretical and experimental tests, the object itself is made on its basis. For instance, the development of new machines, mechanisms, aircraft, buildings, etc., usually pass through the modelling stage.

Models are used fairly extensively in physics, chemistry, cybernetics and biology, and are gradually making their way into social sciences, particularly economics. They help to improve the organisation and management of the economy and certain social processes. Already today mathematical models are successfully used in solving certain economic problems, for example, the optimum distribution of machine loading, rationalisation of transportation, analysis of requirements with the view to improving the supply of commodities to the population, and others.

Editor's Note:

For further study—of social consciousness, its role in the development of society, and forms of social consciousness—as well as a complete presentation of historical materialism, see

V.G. Afanasyev, *Historical Materialism*, ISBN 0-7178-0637-5 $4.95